T0318415

VANET

Intelligent Signal Processing and Data Analysis

Series Editor:
Nilanjan Dey
Department of Information Technology, Techno India College of Technology, Kolkata, India
Proposals for the series should be sent directly to one of the series editors above, or submitted to:
Chapman & Hall/CRC
Taylor and Francis Group
3 Park Square, Milton Park
Abingdon, OX14 4RN, UK

A Beginner's Guide to Image Preprocessing Techniques
Jyotismita Chaki and Nilanjan Dey

Digital Image Watermarking:
Theoretical and Computational Advances
Surekha Borra, Rohit Thanki, and Nilanjan Dey

A Beginner's Guide to Image Shape Feature Extraction Techniques
Jyotismita Chaki and Nilanjan Dey

Coefficient of Variation and Machine Learning Applications
K. Hima Bindu, Raghava Morusupalli, Nilanjan Dey, and C. Raghavendra Rao

Data Analytics for Pandemics:
A COVID-19 Case Study
Gitanjali Rahul Shinde, Asmita Balasaheb Kalamkar, Parikshit N. Mahalle, and Nilanjan Dey

A Beginner's Guide to Multilevel Image Thresholding
Venkatesan Rajinikanth, Nadaradjane Sri Madhava Raja, and Nilanjan Dey

Hybrid Image Processing Methods for Medical Image Examination
Venkatesan Rajinikanth, E Priya, Hong Lin, and Fuhua Lin

Translational Bioinformatics Applications in Healthcare
Khalid Raza and Nilanjan Dey

For more information about this series, please visit: https://www.routledge. com/Intelligent-Signal-Processing-and-Data-Analysis/book-series/INSPDA

VANET
Challenges and Opportunities

Sonali P. Botkar
Sachin P. Godse
Parikshit N. Mahalle
Gitanjali R. Shinde

CRC Press
Taylor & Francis Group
Boca Raton London New York

CRC Press is an imprint of the
Taylor & Francis Group, an **informa** business

First edition published 2021
by CRC Press
6000 Broken Sound Parkway NW, Suite 300, Boca Raton, FL 33487-2742

and by CRC Press
2 Park Square, Milton Park, Abingdon, Oxon, OX14 4RN

© 2021 Sonali P. Botkar, Sachin P. Godse, Parikshit N. Mahalle and Gitanjali Shinde
CRC Press is an imprint of Taylor & Francis Group, an Informa business

No claim to original U.S. Government works

The right of Sonali P. Botkar, Sachin P. Godse, Parikshit N. Mahalle and Gitanjali Shinde to
be identified as author[/s] of this work has been asserted by them in accordance with sections
77 and 78 of the Copyright, Designs and Patents Act 1988.

ISBN-13: 978-0-367-74309-3 (hbk)
ISBN-13: 978-0-367-74312-3 (pbk)

Typeset in Times New Roman
By codeMantra

Contents

Preface

Road transportation is the heart of economic development of a country. Management of traffic services and their effective utilization have a direct impact on successful development of business and other domains in a country. Providing vehicles with communication facility gives ample benefit to overcome many issues on road transportation. It can be used to priorly inform the driver about road condition, traffic jam, accidents happened, weather conditions, front and side distances of other vehicles, sudden break applied by front vehicle, or sudden obstacle in the path. The aforementioned safety information is used for analysis and further to react as per the result of analysis. Along with safety and security of driver, the network facilitates information like map of a city, important locations in the city, paths from the source to the destination, and multimedia data like entertainment movie, etc. VANET (vehicular ad hoc network) research is at the peak, and it has opened various options to the road traffic management and services on road. Developed countries are quite ahead in researching and implementing vehicular network and services. In developing countries like India, this network can be useful to tackle traffic management issue and toll plaza traffic jam by providing an easy way to identify vehicles, deduct toll, and reduce road accidents.

This book provides a journey of VANET development. To establish a VANET network, we should be aware of its basic components, communication medium for network, and different protocols used for communication. The first two chapters provide an introduction of VANET, what is meant by ad hoc network, and discusses about the types of ad hoc networks, comparison of VANET with other ad hoc networks, scenario in VANET, components in VANET, and characteristics of VANET. These chapters also cover different communication methods and protocols used for communication in VANET.

In the vehicular network, messages play important roles compared to any other network as they deal with runtime behaviors on road. As we have seen, there are different types of messages in VANET; it is a challenging task to decide importance of message and to assign priority to it for transmitting messages at the individual node. Chapter 3 gives a relevance-based message forwarding scheme where messages are categorized as per importance. Messages are assigned with priority, and they are transmitted based on their trust value and relevance value.

VANET is the most volatile and open network; there is no any control on the movement of nodes in a network. A new node can easily enter into the network, which may raise a security issue. Due to this feature, VANET is prone to many challenges like volatility, critical time latency of messages delivery, high mobility of nodes, VANET security, efficient message forwarding, and mitigation techniques to address VANET security. These challenges are discussed in Chapter 4. To understand VANET, various real-time applications and projects are explained in Chapter 5. The book is summarized in Chapter 6, which also covers future outlook of VANET in developed and developing countries.

CONCLUDING REMARK

To understand the basic terminology, component, characteristics, and challenges in VANET, this book will be the one-place solution.

The main characteristics of this book are as follows:

- Covers all important concepts of VANET for beginners.
- Considers different road scenarios in VANET.
- Covers essential communication protocols in VANET.
- Introduces approaches for VANET implementation using simulator.
- Provides in detail the classification of messages and priority-based message forwarding strategy.
- Gives a separate chapter on different applications of VANET.

This book is useful for undergraduates, postgraduates, industry, researchers, and research scholars in ICT, and we are sure that this book will be well received by all stakeholders.

Authors

Prof. Sonali P. Botkar obtained her B.E. degree in E&TC Engineering from NDMVP, Savitribai Phule Pune University, Pune, India, and M.E. in E&TC (signal Processing) from MKSSS's Cummins College of Engineering for Women, Savitribai Phule University, Pune, India. Her areas of interest are mobile ad hoc network, wireless sensor network, and cognitive radio network. She has published more than 15 papers in international and national journals and conferences. She has authored one book. She has one patent to her credit. Currently, she is working as Assistant Professor in Vishwakarma University, Pune, India. She can be reached at: sonali.botkar@vupune.ac.in.

Dr. Sachin P. Godse obtained his B.E. degree in Computer Engineering from Pune University, India, in 2005, and M.E. degree in Computer Science and Engineering from Savitribai Phule Pune University, Pune, India. He completed his Ph.D. in Computer Science and Engineering from Savitribai Phule Pune University, Pune, India. His areas of interest are vehicular ad hoc network, mobile ad hoc network, natural language processing, object-oriented programming, object-oriented modeling, and software engineering. He has more than 14 years of teaching and research experience. He has published more than 22 research publications at national and international journals and conferences. He has authored 11 books. He has two patents to his credit. He can be reached at: sachin.gds@gmail.com.

Dr. Parikshit N. Mahalle obtained his B.E. degree in Computer Science and Engineering from Sant Gadge Baba Amravati University, Amravati, India, and M.E. degree in Computer Engineering from Savitribai Phule Pune University, Pune, India. He completed his Ph.D. in Computer Science and Engineering specialization in Wireless Communication from Aalborg University, Aalborg, Denmark. He has more than 18 years of teaching and research experience. He has published more than 130 research publications at national and international journals and conferences. He has four edited books to his credit by Springer, De Gruyter, and CRC presses. He has seven patents to his credit. He has authored ten books. He has 993 citations and 12 h-indexes. He can be reached at: aalborg.pnm@gmail.com.

Dr. Gitanjali R. Shinde obtained her B.E. in Computer Science and Engineering from Pune University, India, in 2006, with first class with distinction, and M.E. degree in Computer Engineering from Savitribai Phule Pune University, Pune, India. She completed her Ph.D. in Computer Science and Engineering from Aalborg University, Copenhagen, Denmark. She has more than 11 years of teaching and research experience. She has published more than 40 research publications at national and international journals and conferences. She has edited books to her credit by De Gruyter press. She has authored two books. She can be reached at: gr8gita@gmail.com.

Introduction to VANET 1

1.1 VANET BASICS

Before starting technical stuff in vehicular ad hoc network (VANET), it is important to see the evolution of wireless communication in short. Wireless communication is a turning point in communication network, which makes many tasks simpler. Due to wireless communication, people can communicate their data on wireless medium, i.e., air. Wireless communication utilizes different signals like radio wave, microwave, ultrasonic wave, and infrared wave. There is no need of physical mediums like wire and optical fiber, which makes communication easy. Devices investigated in the 19th and 20th centuries, like computer, pager, and mobile phone, use a wireless medium of communication and have a capability of anytime, anywhere communication facility. Wireless communication network is further extended with the feature called mobility. Mobility means that nodes in networks are moving with different speeds and establish communication with other nodes. Wireless networks are with access points and routers as forwarding devices that are located at different places. Wireless ad hoc networks are without access points and routers.

1.1.1 Introduction to Ad Hoc Network

Ad hoc network is a temporary network, which is established for emergency situation on demand when there is no infrastructure and no sufficient time to build a network. This network plays an important role in situations like disaster, battle field, earthquake, and remote location. It becomes easy to establish a communication using ad hoc network. The following are important features of an ad hoc network.

1.1.1.1 Ad Hoc Network Features

- **Infrastructureless network:** Like other network, it doesn't require centralized controlling authority, routers, and physical medium for transmitting data.
- **Nodes in the network can be mobile:** Nodes can be stationary or nodes in the network have freedom to move in the communication range of network nodes. If all nodes are moving with a constant speed in the range of each other, connection can remain without interruption. In some cases, every node moves at a different speed, which can be connected and disconnected from the network.
- **Each node acts as a router and takes the decision of forwarding the packets:** Nodes in the network themselves play a role of router. Nodes either send their own messages or forward another node messages to destination nodes. Route-finding process is initiated when a particular message is sent by the source node. Nodes in the network have individual or group strategy for forwarding messages.
- **No centralized controlling authority:** In other wireless network, behaviors of nodes in the network are controlled by centralized controlling authority. In the case of ad hoc network, there is no centralized controlling authority.
- **Flexible in nature, can establish, and can dissolve as nodes move:** As nodes in the network can move, they result in formation and deformation of network from time to time.
- **Network topology changes from time to time as nodes move:** If ad hoc network nodes are movable, it can result in a change in topology from time to time.
- **Hop-to-hop communication is possible:** Nodes in the network are working themselves like a router; therefore, hop-to-hop communication is possible. If two nodes are not in the range of each other, they can establish communication using intermediate nodes.

1.1.2 Classifications of Ad Hoc Networks

Ad hoc network is classified into the following types (Figure 1.1):

- **Mobile ad hoc network:** It is a self-organizing ad hoc network. In this network, nodes are nothing but mobile devices. Nodes are connected wirelessly to other nodes. Depending on the range of individual node, communication can be established (Figure 1.2).

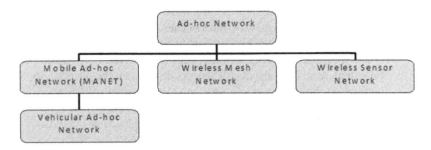

FIGURE 1.1   Classification of ad hoc networks.

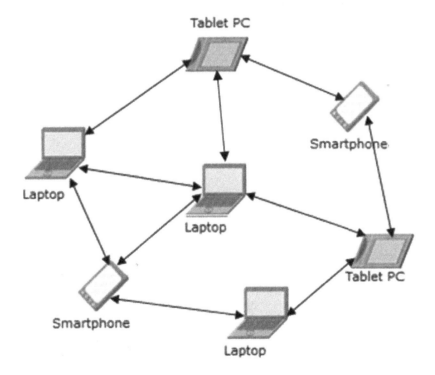

FIGURE 1.2   Mobile ad hoc network.

- **Wireless mesh network:** It is the simplest form of a wireless network. It is also called mesh network because nodes are connected to each other by mesh topology. The nodes in the networks are devices like laptops, mobile phones, and other wireless equipment.

Wireless devices are communicating with each other using network devices like routers, gateway, and switches (Figure 1.3).

- **Wireless sensor network:** Sensor network is a wireless network. Nodes in the networks are different sensors that sense environmental parameters. The selection of sensors depends on the purpose of application. Some commonly used applications employing sensors are to detect pressure, temperature, humidity, distance, sound, etc. This network is static network as nodes are deployed at fixed distances. The main tasks of sensor nodes are to collect data from specific environment and pass to actuators, where the collected data is processed. Based on the analysis of processing data, decision is taken. As per decision made by the control unit, action takes place

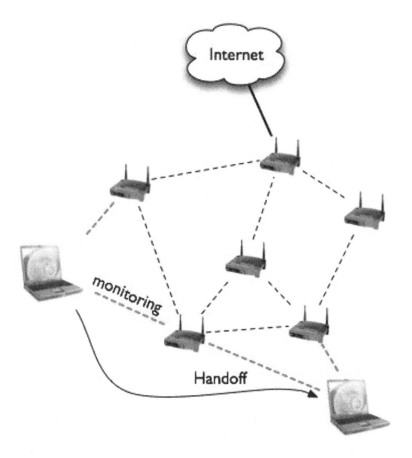

FIGURE 1.3 Wireless mesh network.

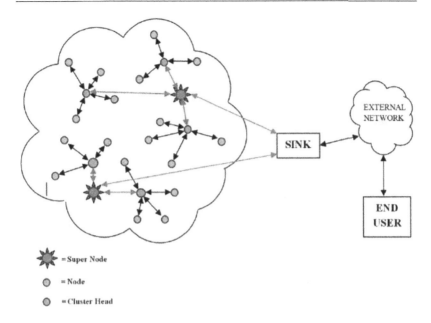

= Super Node

= Node

= Cluster Head

FIGURE 1.4   Wireless sensor network.

by the respective unit. Figure 1.4 shows the wireless sensor network architecture. It is a cluster-based network; each cluster consists of member nodes and cluster head. Sensor nodes communicate with cluster head, and the cluster head is connected with super node. All super nodes are connected with sink. Sink receives data from sensor nodes and transmits it to an external network for processing.

- **Vehicular ad hoc network:** It is a subtype of mobile ad hoc network (MANET). Nodes in network are vehicles and road side unit (RSU) deployed along road side. It is highly dynamic network as the vehicles are moving with a speed of 40–200 km/hr.

1.1.3 Vehicular Ad Hoc Network (VANET)

Communication network has become a wide service domain in all fields of human beings. It is because of the latest innovation in automated electronic devices and their controlling software packages. Human beings started their journey of communication from landline telephone, and now, it reached at entity communication, i.e., Internet of Things. As objects in the real world started communication with each other, it motivated finding solutions on traffic management by using vehicular networks. In these networks, nodes are

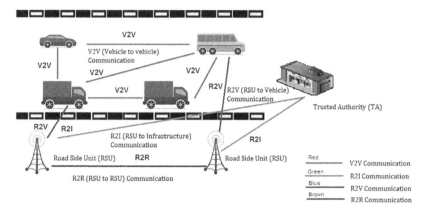

FIGURE 1.5 Vehicular ad hoc network.

nothing but moving vehicles on road. These vehicles share different information with each other through a wireless medium. In recent days, VANET has become a challenging and interesting area of research for researchers.

Figure 1.5 shows a VANET scenario in which nodes in the network are vehicles and RSUs along the road. Four different types of communications are shown in this figure. The red line shows the vehicle-to-vehicle communication; the green line shows the RSU-to-infrastructure communication, and vice versa; the blue line shows the vehicle-to-RSU communication, and vice versa; and the brown line shows the RSU-to-RSU communication.

1.1.4 Differences between VANET and MANET

- **Mobility** is high in VANET as compared to that in MANET, because vehicles are moving with a speed of 40–200 km/hr.
- **Cost** of VANET is high compared to that of MANET. Vehicles are deployed with on-board units (OBUs). Vehicles are connected with longer-distance vehicles through RSUs. Depending on the configuration and ranges of OBUs and RSUs, the cost of the network may vary.
- **Communication range of nodes** in VANET is wider than that of nodes in MANET.
- **Frequency band** assigned for VANET communication is 5.86–5.92 GHz, while for MANET, the frequency band is 2.4–5.2 GHz.
- **Density of network** is higher in VANET than in MANET, and it may vary according to the mobility of vehicles.

TABLE 1.1 Comparison between VANET and MANET

PARAMETER	VANET	MANET
Mobility	High	Low
Cost	High	Low
Communication range of nodes	Vehicle: 100–400 m RSU: 1–14 km	10–100 m
Frequencies band	5.86–5.92 GHz	2.4–5.2 GHz
Network density	High and varies from time to time	Low
Node lifetime	Depends on the lifetime of vehicle	Depends on the lifetime of node battery
Channel bandwidth	1–40 MHz	10–20 MHz
Volatility	High	Low

- As vehicles' **battery life** is longer, nodes survive for a longer time till the life of vehicles. Nodes in MANET suffer from battery life problem.
- **Bandwidth of channel** used in VANET is 1–40 MHz, which is larger than the bandwidth of channel used in MANET, i.e., 10–20 MHz.
- VANET is a more **volatile network** as compared to MANET due to the speed of nodes.

Table 1.1 gives a comparison between VANET and MANET [1].

1.2 VANET SCENARIOS

Depending on road types like single lane, two lanes, multilane, one way, two ways, and cross roads, vehicle directions and network topology can be changed. Let's see different scenarios of VANET.

1.2.1 Single-Lane One-Directional Vehicle Flow

Consider a normal road scenario where single road with one-way transportation is allowed and all vehicles are traveling in one direction. RSUs are deployed along the road side. During one-directional flow of vehicles, there is less possibility of connection disturbance.

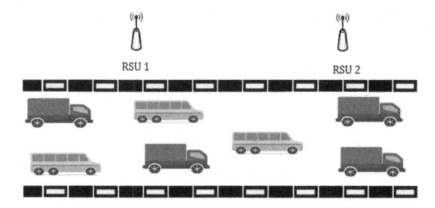

FIGURE 1.6   One-lane one-directional vehicle flow.

Figure 1.6 shows the single-lane one-directional vehicle flow, in which vehicles are moving in one direction that is left to right.

1.2.2 Two-Lane Two-Directional Vehicle Flow

In this scenario, vehicles are flowing in two lanes and in two different directions (exactly opposite to each other). In this type of vehicle transportation, vehicles in the opposite direction remain in the vicinity of each other for a short time period. So in such cases, if we establish separate networks for nodes (vehicles) in the same direction, then it will give better performance. Two lanes are treated separately with a separate set of RSUs for each lane, which will reduce the possibility of connection disturbance.

Figure 1.7 shows two separate lanes for vehicles. In lane 1, vehicles are moving from left to right, while in lane 2, vehicles are moving from right to left; i.e., vehicles in lanes 1 and 2 are moving in exactly opposite direction.

1.2.3 Multilane Multidirectional Vehicle Flow

In the case of express highways, the number of lanes is more than two for one-sided vehicle transportation. Multidirectional flow means that vehicles are moving in either forward direction, opposite direction, or left and right directions.

Figure 1.8 shows a road crossover where four lanes meet. It is a multilane multidirectional scenario. Vehicles are moving in four different directions.

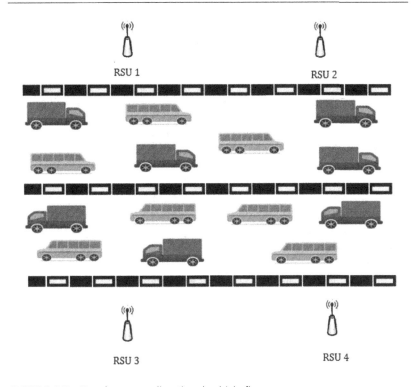

FIGURE 1.7 Two-lane two-directional vehicle flows.

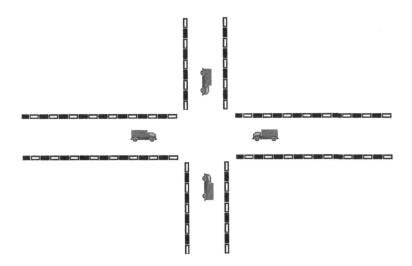

FIGURE 1.8 Multilane multidirectional vehicle flows.

1.3 NEED OF VANET

Transportation is the backbone of economy in any country. Along with basic infrastructures like roads and vehicles, it is important to control the vehicles on road intelligently. Traditional traffic management systems used traffic signals for monitoring and controlling traffic on road. Traffic signals with three colors, i.e., red, green, and yellow, are time-based functioning device. Sometimes, it causes unnecessary waiting even there are no vehicles passing at the cross road. Waiting will cause congestion of vehicles and wastage of time. There is a need of some smart solution for traffic control where traffic information can be shared with other vehicles and the signal controller. VANET and vehicles can share important information about traffic jam, path, map, weather conditions, road conditions, drivers' behaviors, information request, alternative paths, etc.

Drastically increasing numbers of vehicles on road is the biggest issue all over the world. It also increases the traffic management overload. It is very difficult to control road traffic using human-oriented traffic management system. Hence, there is a need of automation; VANET have the ability to automate the traffic management system. The number of road accidents and deaths that occur in those accidents is also one of the big issues in road transportation. If drivers can get necessary control information priorly, they can take necessary actions to avoid the accidents. There is a need of VANET to provide the best solution on all issues and to achieve comfortable, safe, and intelligent driving for vehicle drivers. VANET provides an intelligent transportation system (ITS). In this vehicular network, vehicles have the facility to receive and send messages. Vehicles will get emergency messages related to traffic jam, an accident that has happened on the road, bad weather, bad road condition, locations, paths, etc. in advance through a wireless medium. Vehicle can also request for information like path, map, and multimedia data. It is an amazing experience which makes driving comfortable and will also avoid accidents and wastage of time.

1.4 COMPONENTS OF VANET

1.4.1 Vehicle with On-Board Unit (OBU)

Smart transport system (STS) or VANET is only possible because of the devices called "on-board units" (OBUs). OBUs provide processing of their own vehicle data, traffic data, and other vehicle-related data, and thus help to take a decision in various real-life applications like congestion control and accidents prevention. To make VANET environment reality, all vehicles should be loaded with devices that are low-cost and easily available technologies, and satisfy the technical requirements to become a part of an STS. To fulfill these requirements, academics and researchers have come up with devices like OBUs. Nowadays, all vehicles in the STS come up with inbuilt new-generation OBUs which help in fulfilling traveling needs, traffic management, emergency management, and toll management with more flexible and scalable installations with very low interventions in civil infrastructures.

The STS Standardization Committee defined certain objectives, system requirements, and characteristics that should be incorporated into every OBU.

1. **Objectives:**
   - **Vehicle location tracking:** An OBU should track the position of the vehicle (longitude and latitude) and the distance it travels.
   - **Intervehicular communication:** An OBU should provide a connection with other OBUs and RSUs.
   - **Vehicle-to-infrastructure communication:** An OBU should make available communication with a trusted authority (TA).
   - **Acquire vehicle and traffic data, and pass on to various applications:** An OBU should collect different parameters through sensors deployed on vehicles and provide decisions after processing to various applications.
   - **Various kinds of interface support like USB, RS232, and Wi-Fi:** An OBU should support various communication interfaces for interaction with internal vehicle application and outside world.

2. **System requirements:**
   - Design of OBU and its integration
   - Easy and flexible data acquisition with various means
   - Hardware and software support
   - Cost-effective.

3. **OBU architecture:** The OBU architecture consists of four parts:
   - **Data acquisition:** Data are collected from various inbuilt sensors, such as traffic data and mobility data which self-possessed by the vehicular network.
   - **Network communication:** Using wireless sensors, network data are forwarded to various VANET nodes like RSUs or servers.

- **Data binding and decision-making:** Event detection, priority decision, and authentication like decisions are taken using this part.
- **Pass on data to applications:** All the data are passed to the application layer. And various applications use this data to accomplish objectives of different applications.

The layered architecture of OBU is given in Figure 1.9.

1. **Low-level architecture:** An OBU is integrated into the vehicles, and it helps to communicate V2V or V2I in VANET. It consists of a processor, a transmitter, a receiver, a memory, sensors, a UI, and a network interface [2]. The low-level OBU architecture is shown in Figure 1.10.
   - **Core computation:** Gathers data so that the real-time applications can be performed as required.
   - **Memory:** Stores data like vehicle data and event data, which can be processed for further communication.

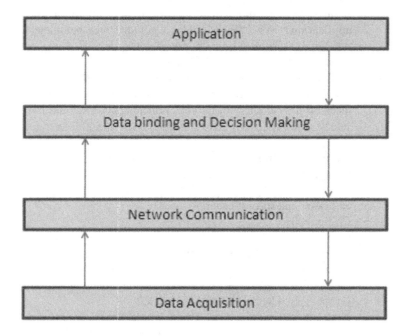

FIGURE 1.9 OBU architecture.

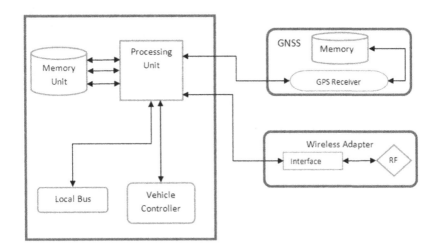

FIGURE 1.10   OBU block diagram.

- **GPS equipment:** Tracks own position to run location-based services.
- **Wireless communication:** Allows communication between V2V and V2I.
- **Operating system:** Embedded operative system software.
2. **Latest OBU specifications:** The latest OBU specifications used in VANET environments are shown in Table 1.2. It also gives hardware components present in OBUs and their configurations.

1.4.2 Road Side Unit (RSU)

V2V communication is like one-to-one communication in VANET, and this is possible because of inbuilt Wi-Fi devices. But when a vehicle wants to communicate out-of-range vehicles or get events that occurred far away, point-to-point or local communication is not useful; hence, the vehicle should use V2I communication. So, RSUs work along with OBUs and other infrastructures to enhance the VANET communication capabilities of all vehicles.

1. **Role of RSU:** RSUs are deployed in such environment where they help to extend vehicle coverage and network performance in a VANET [3,4]. The following are some roles of RSUs:

TABLE 1.2   Latest OBU specifications

COMPONENT	DESCRIPTION
Processor	800-MHz iMX6 Dual Core
Memory	Up to 4-GB DDR3 DRAM *1 GB DDR3 Standard
Storage	Up to 16-GB Flash * GB Standard
Radio	Dual DSRC, Wi-Fi/BT
GPS	U-BIOX. Tracking sensitivity: −160 dBm
Secure flash	Provided by Infineon HSM SL197
Temperature	−40 C to +85 C
Antenna/GPS connectors	Fakra type Z/C
Other interfaces	CAN, 2 USB, MicroSD, serial, Ethernet
Standard compliance	802.11P, IEEE1609.X, and SAE J2735(2015), J2945
Security	1609.2, IPSec & SSL
Enclosure	140×133×42 (L×W×H)
Power management	Optional battery backup for a range of functionality
Power	9–30 V DC
Power consumption	Nominal<5 W, Max 10 W

- Message delivery to vehicles
- Forwarding message to other vehicles
- Internet access to vehicles
- Interface between vehicle and trusted authority server (TAS)
- Extended range.

2. **RSU architecture:** An RSU architecture with its different components is shown in Figure 1.11. It consists of RSU side request and response channels. Received requests are scheduled for service as per the scheduler mechanism [5].

3. **RSU architectures components:**
   - **Request channel queue:** Whenever an RSU receives packets from vehicles, it first moves to RqCQ, and as per priority, it gets processed by the RSU.
   - **Reply channel queue:** Reply packets are getting stored in RpCQ, and as per priority, they are forwarded to other vehicles or RSUs.
   - **Scheduler:** This helps a VANET to manage packet priority and handle emergency messages or events.

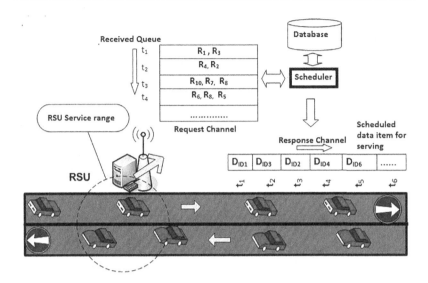

FIGURE 1.11   RSU architecture.

- **Memory:** To store packets data, authentication data, and other data as per applications.
- **Network:** To communicate between vehicles, other RSUs, and TASs.
- **Decision module:** It receives the packets, and as per application requirements, it processes the data and takes decisions that suit applications.

4. **Latest RSU specifications:** The latest RSU specifications with its hardware components are shown in Table 1.3.

1.4.3 Trusted Authority Server (TAS)

TAS is nothing but the main server to keep records of VANET like all RSUs, vehicles, and OBUs. Also, it is responsible to authorize these RSUs and vehicles; after that only, RSUs or vehicles can communicate in a vehicular network.

This provides the secure communication services to RSUs and vehicles in a VANET system. In small infrastructures, only one TA can be deployed, but in large environments, many TAs are deployed. In most of the cases, TAs are deployed in hierarchical TA system, where multiple TAs are deployed under one TA and so on [6].

TABLE 1.3 Latest RSU specifications

COMPONENT	DESCRIPTION
Processor	800-Mhz, iMX6 dual core
Memory	4-GB DDR DRAM
Storage	8-GB Flash
DSRC interface	Dual radio support
C-2V2X interfaces	PC-5 (Qualcomm MDM 9150)
GNSS	Multi-Constellation, −160 db sensitivity
HSM	Infineon SLI 97
Power rating	IEEE 802.3 at PoE
Power consumption	< 10W
Temperature	−35 C to +75 C
Dimensions	8″ (L)×8.5″″(H)×2.3/4″ (D)
Antenna connectors	N-Type Male (V2XRadio) & SMA (GNSS) Wi-Fi (built-in)
LEDs	Power, Satus, & Diag
Standards compliance	USDOT RSU v4.1a specification* (Full compliance for DSRC) only)
FCC compliance	FCC, CFR 47 Part 90* (DSRC only)
Traffic controller compatibility	Multiple traffic controllers
Installation kit (included)	Pole mounting kit
Accessory kit (optional)	PoE (Power Over Ethernet) controller
Standard support	IEEE 802.11P-2012, IEEE 1609.2-2016, IEEE 1609.3-2016

1. **Role of TA:**
   - Verify state-level trusted authority (STA) and city-level trusted authority (CTA), RSUs, and vehicles
   - Centralized authentication system
   - Centralized registration system for RSUs and OBUs.

2. **TA architecture**: As shown in Figure 1.12, this is a hierarchical TA system where TA works as a central TA; STA works as a state-level trust authority which works under TA; and CTA is a city-level trust authority which works under STA. And every CTA communicates with many immediate connected RSUs. Every TA verifies STA, and every STA verifies CTA.

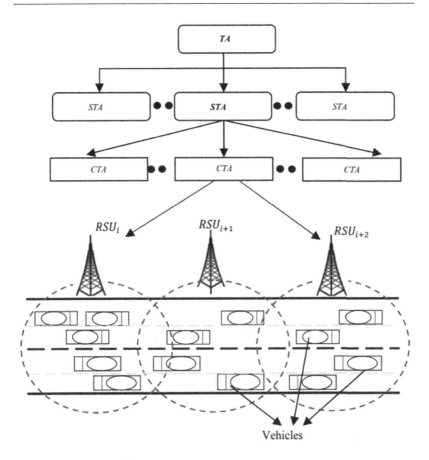

FIGURE 1.12 TA architecture.

1.4.4 Event Data Recorder (EDR)

It is a device deployed on vehicle which keeps the track of messages transferred from or received by vehicles. Record can be further used for the analysis of an event.

1.4.5 Global Positioning System

It is a device that keeps the track of location and respective time stamp of a vehicle. It also provides the facility of map and navigation.

1.4.6 Radars and Sensors

Radar is a device on the vehicle. It detects any obstacle on the road while vehicle is running. It helps to avoid accidents. Various sensors are deployed on the vehicles for sensing environmental parameters (such as temperature, humidity, wind pressure, and fog) and send this information to computing unit to make analysis.

1.4.7 Computing Device

It receives data from various sensors, digital cameras, radars, and transceivers present on the vehicle. It also receives messages from RSUs or other vehicles. These data are processed by a computing device for taking necessary decisions.

1.4.8 Electronic License Plate

It is unique identity, i.e., vehicle number assigned by the certification authority during the registration phase of the network.

1.5 CHARACTERISTICS OF VANET

1.5.1 Infrastructureless

VANET is an infrastructureless network, if we consider the network that is formed by vehicles. There is no need of any physical medium between vehicles for communication. There is no need of any centralized controlling authority. As hop-to-hop communication is possible in VANET, there is no need of hardware devices like switches or hubs. Even if we consider RSUs and TAs in the network, these are very basic resources which are deployed along the road side during the construction of roads by the road authority in foreign countries.

1.5.2 Self-Organized

Nodes in VANET takes their own decisions for forwarding messages. Nodes itself act as a switch for transferring data. Hop-to-hop communication is possible. These features make VANET as a self-organized network.

1.5.3 Distributed Network

VANET with vehicles, RSUs, and TAs forms a distributed network. TAs are the topmost controllers. These does the registration of vehicles and RSUs in the initial phase of the network. Under a TA, different RSUs are deployed along the road side. RSUs are regional authorities providing services to vehicles coming under their regions. This forms a scenario of distributed network.

1.5.4 Highly Dynamic Nodes

As vehicles in VANET are moving in high speeds from 60 to 200 km/hr, it is a highly dynamic network with high-mobility nodes [7].

1.5.5 Predictable Topology (Using Digital Map)

VANET uses a mesh topology for communication as nodes are moving randomly. If a digital map is used to trace the runtime location and time of vehicles, we can predict the topology. The digital map is very similar to Google map, which gives runtime locations of vehicles with respect to time. We can easily predict the future topology between the nodes by the current location and speed of the vehicle [8].

1.5.6 Critical Latency Requirement

Latency is nothing but the time interval between sending messages by a source node and receiving messages by a receiver node. In a VANET, due to highly mobile nodes, i.e., vehicles, they may be running in opposite directions. The nodes remain in the vicinity of each other for very short time periods. It is important to receive the message by the destination vehicle in a given time period. To achieve this network, a critical latency requirement is needed. Communication in the VANET network should be made with low latency.

1.5.7 No Power Constraint

Nodes in VANET are vehicles. The life of nodes is nothing but the life of vehicles. In comparison with other networks like MANET and sensor network, VANET nodes do not suffer from battery life power problems [4,8,9].

1.6 SUMMARY

This chapter gives an introduction to ad hoc networks and their classification. It also provides a detailed introduction to the VANET and its components, different scenarios, challenges, communication types, and characteristics.

REFERENCES

1. R. Nirmala and R. Sudha, "A relativity cram between MANET and VANET background along routing protocol", *International Journal of Advanced Information Science and Technology(IJAIST)*, vol. 26, no. 26, pp. 153–157, June 2014.
2. M. Petracca, P. Pagano, R. Pelliccia, et al., "On board unit hardware and software design for vehicular ad-hoc Networks", *Roadside Networks for Vehicular Communications: Architectures, Applications and Test Fields* (Eds. R. Daher, A. Vinel), pp. 38–56. IGI Global, 2013).
3. H. Hartenstein and K. P. Laberteaux, *VANETs: Vehicular Applications and Inter-Networking Technologies*, Wiley, UK, 2010.
4. F. Aadil, S. Rizwan and A. Akram, "Vehicular Ad Hoc Networks (VANETs), Past Present and Future: A survey," *In HET-NETs, The Seventh International Working*, England, UK, 2013.
5. G. G. Md. Nawaz Ali and E. Chan, "Co-operative load balancing in multiple road side units (RSUs)- based vehicular ad hoc networks (VANETs)", *International Journal of Wireless Networks and Broadband Technologies*, vol. 1, no. 4, pp. 1–21, 2011.
6. B.K. Chaurasia, S. Verma, et al., "Infrastructure based authentication in VANETs", *International Journal of Multimedia and Ubiquitous Engineering*, vol. 6, no. 2, pp. 41–54, April, 2011.
7. K. Ravi "AODV routing in VANET for message authentication using ECDSA", *IEEE Conference on Communications and Signal Processing (ICCSP)*, pp. 1389–1393, 2014.
8. S. Al-Sultan, M.M. Al-Doori, et al., "A comprehensive survey on vehicular Ad Hoc network", *Journal of Network and Computer Applications*, vol. 37, pp. 380–392. Elsevier, February 2013.
9. M. S. Anwer and C. Guy, "A survey of VANETs technologies", *Journal of Emerging Trends in Computing and Information Sciences*, vol. 5, no. 4, 2014.

Communication in VANET

2

2.1 TYPES OF COMMUNICATION IN VANET

Communication in a VANET (vehicular ad hoc network) differs from that of other ad hoc networks. Vehicles moving on the road and road side units (RSUs) along the roads are nodes in the VANET. Communication hierarchy in vehicular communication is shown in Figure 2.1; the topmost authority is TA (trusted authority), which does the registration of all vehicles and RSUs in the network at the initial phase of network. It controls all RSUs under its range. RSUs are deployed region-wise providing the services to vehicles under its region.

As per the nature, range, and types of nodes, communication in VANET is categorized into vehicle to RSU (V2R), vehicle to vehicle (V2V), RSU to RSU

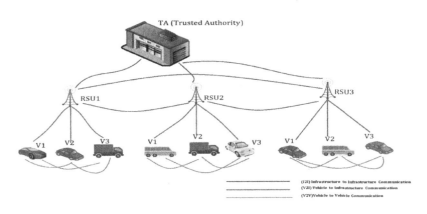

FIGURE 2.1 Communication hierarchy in VANET.

(R2R), RSU to TA (R2T), and TA to TA (T2T) [1,2]. Different types of communication in VANET are explained in detail in the following subsections.

2.1.1 Vehicle-to-Vehicle Communication

If we consider vehicle-to-vehicle communication, it is fully an ad hoc network. One vehicle can communicate to other vehicles if it is in the communication range. Vehicle-to-vehicle communication uses a wireless medium like dedicated short-range communication (DSRC), Wi-Fi, or Bluetooth. If two vehicles are not in the range of each other, but under the same RSU, then they can establish communication using a hop-to-hop communication. Node in the vehicular network acts as a router; therefore, the hop-to-hop communication is possible.

If a vehicle under the range of RSU1 wants to communicate with a vehicle under the range of RSU2, the vehicle communicates through its RSU to other RSU followed by the other vehicle. A scenario of vehicle-to-vehicle communication is depicted in Figure 2.2.

2.1.2 Vehicle-to-RSU/Vehicle-to-Infrastructure Communication

Vehicle-to-RSU communication is also called as vehicle-to-infrastructure communication. Vehicle-to-RSU communication is initiated when a vehicle enters into RSU range. The vehicle makes a service request by passing a

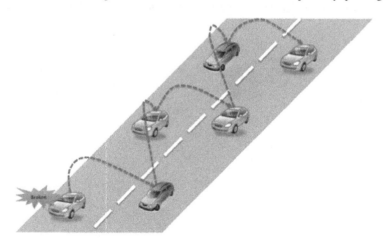

FIGURE 2.2 Vehicle-to-vehicle communication.

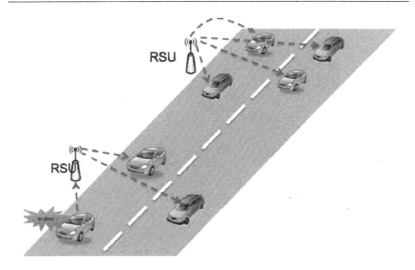

FIGURE 2.3 Vehicle-to-RSU communication.

request message to RSU. This type of communication also takes place when the vehicle wants to communicate with a vehicle that resides in the range of another RSU. RSUs also communicate with vehicles in their range, in order to pass control signals. As vehicles are moving and RSUs are stationary, this type of communication is called partially ad hoc. Vehicle-to-RSU communication uses a wireless medium like DSRC, Wi-Fi, or Bluetooth. Hop-to-hop communication is allowed. A scenario of vehicle-to-RSU communication is shown in Figure 2.3.

2.1.3 RSU-to-RSU Communication

An RSU communicates with another RSU in the network for various purposes (like to pass emergency information about bad weather, to cross-check log of vehicles, to intimate about accident, or traffic jam). This is purely a static network as there are no moving nodes. The RSU in this network communicates with the other RSU through either a wired or wireless medium (Figure 2.4).

2.1.4 RSU-to-TA Communication

An RSU communicates to a TA, when a vehicle is authenticated by the RSU first time; it is a static network. The TA also communicates some emergency messages or traffic-related policies to all RSUs. The TA regulates activities of

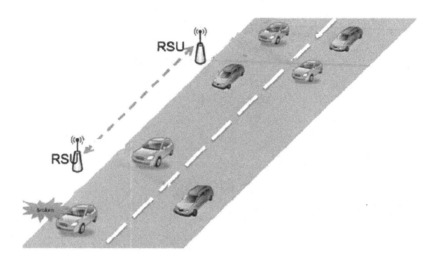

FIGURE 2.4 RSU-to-RSU communication.

all RSUs by passing messages from time to time. Communication takes place through either a wired or wireless medium (Figure 2.5).

2.1.5 TA-to-TA Communication

If a region is geographically spread over longer distances, then single TA is not sufficient to control the network activity over the whole region. In this case, regions are separated as per the capacity of TA and the whole portion may be divided into required regions. Each region is controlled by one TA. In the above scenario, one TA can communicate to another TA for sharing common information. They may request data of RSUs or vehicles from other regions. TA-to-TA communication takes place through a wired medium (Figure 2.6).

2.1.6 Communication Ranges and Frequencies in VANET

As a vehicular network is spread over a large geographical area, its communication range requirement is more as compared to other ad hoc networks. As we have seen, there are different types of communications in VANET.

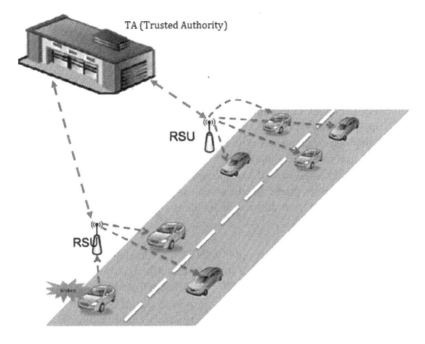

FIGURE 2.5   RSU-to-TA communication.

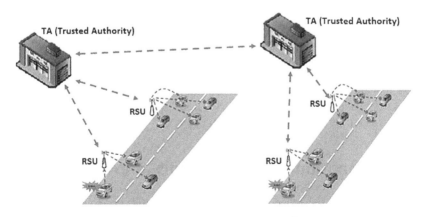

FIGURE 2.6   TA-to-TA communication.

a. Vehicle-to-vehicle communication range using DSRC is from 100 to 1000 m; i.e., a vehicle is in the range of 100–1000 m distance from the another vehicle.

b. Vehicle-to-RSU communication range using DSRC is the same as 100–1000 m; i.e., a vehicle can send messages to an RSU which is in the range of 100–1000 m distance from the vehicle.

c. RSU-to-RSU communication range using a wired or wireless medium is 1–14 km; i.e., RSUs within 1–14 km distance from each other can communicate with each other.

d. As hop-to-hop communication is possible in VANET, vehicles under the same RSU but not in the range of each other can communicate through intermediate vehicles.

e. Two vehicles from different RSU areas can communicate through RSUs.

Frequencies in VANET: Nodes in a VANET are vehicles and RSUs. Nodes, i.e., vehicles, are moving in a high speed, nearly 40–200 km/hr. High speeds of nodes require low latency in V2V and V2R communications. Latency is the time interval between sending messages by a sender node and receiving message by a receiver node. It should be very low. To achieve the low latency requirement in VANET, the speed of data transmission should be high. High-speed data transmission needs special high-frequency ranges like frequencies used in satellite communication. Considering special frequency requirement of VANET, the IEEE 802.11 standards are modified to new standard known as IEEE 802.11p. This standard is based on the 802.11a technology and is also referred as the DSRC standard. DSRC is based on the 5-GHz frequency spectrum, which is further divided into seven channels. The frequency of each channel is 10 MHz. Out of these seven channels, one is control channel (CCH) and six are service channels (SCHs). Figure 2.7 shows the frequencies and channels used for different message forwarding strategies in VANET.

CCH is dedicated to transmit network management messages. Network management messages include messages like resource reservation and topology management. CCH is also used to transmit high-priority messages like road safety and emergency messages. SCHs are dedicated to different service-related data transmission.

2.1.7 Communication Protocols in VANET

As compared to the other wireless network, VANET has some additional requirements to establish the communication in network. A VANET network should satisfy requirements such as latency, bandwidth, error rate, and

Channel Type	Channel No	Frequency Ranges
Accident Avoidance Safety of life	CHANNEL 172	5860 MHz
Service channels	CHANNEL 174	5870 MHz
Service channels	CHANNEL 176	5880 MHz
Control Channel	CHANNEL 178	5890 MHz
Service Channels	CHANNEL 180	5900 MHz
Service Channels	CHANNEL 182	5910 MHz
High Power Long Range	CHANNEL 184	5920 MHz

FIGURE 2.7   Frequencies available in 802.11p.

coverage area. Initially, VANET communication is experimented with some extension in IEEE 802.11 (Wireless LAN). IEEE 802.11 provides 1–2 Mbps in the 2.4-GHz frequency range. However, the requirement of VANET is 100–1000 Mbps with a frequency range of 5.8–5.9 GHz. The existing IEEE 802.11 protocol is extended to IEEE 802.11P, which is also called as DSRC.

2.2 INTRODUCTION TO DEDICATED SHORT-RANGE COMMUNICATION (DSRC)

Wireless access for vehicular environment (WAVE) is a specially designed standard for DSRC. It is an extension of IEEE 802.11 (Wi-Fi). Different services provided by WAVE are given in Table 2.1 [3,4].

TABLE 2.1   WAVE standards

WAVE STANDARDS	SERVICE PROVIDED
IEEE 1609.0	WAVE architecture
IEEE 1609.1	Network resources management
IEEE 1609.2	Provide security services
IEEE 1609.3	Networking services
IEEE 1609.4	Multichannel operations

Introduction to IEEE 1609 (WAVE) family:

These standards are specially designed for vehicular network to satisfy the requirements of the vehicular network. WAVE family provides different standards and protocols to offer and maintain different services in VANET. IEEE1609 family along with IEEE 802.11P do different tasks, which are required under physical layer to application layer.

Due to dynamic nature of vehicles, it is a volatile network. Low latency is an important requirement of the vehicular network. To achieve low latency, communication speed should be greater than that of normal wireless and ad hoc network. This high-speed range for the vehicular network is from 6 to 27 Mbps, and the communication range is up to 1000 m. RSUs deployed along road side, OBU (on-board unit) deployed on vehicles, and WAVE interfaces constitute the backbone of VANET.

Table 2.1 gives different standards used to provide high-speed communication, management of network, and security for network communication. IEEE 1609.0 gives the architecture for WAVE. IEEE 1609.1 provides the network resource management functionality. IEEE 1609.2 gives the security protocols for communication and authentication of different nodes and resources. IEEE 1609.3 defines the different protocol for network management. Physical channel access is defined in 802.11P. WAVE services are divided into two channels, namely, CCH and SCH. Communication channels available for different services in VANET are shown in Figure 2.7.

The link bandwidth of CCH and SCH is further divided into transmission cycles. Each cycle consists of a control frame and a service frame. Frame duration is 50 ms for control or service frame. The performance of DSRC is investigated by researcher for different application services in the vehicular environment. Investigation of research shows that DSRC is most reliable in vehicle-to-vehicle communication.

2.2.1 IEEE 1609.0 (WAVE Architecture)

IEEE 1609.0 provides an architecture for WAVE. As shown in figure, it gives different layer like basic ISO-OSI model of communication. The bottom-most layer is physical layer (IEEE 802.11P) in VANET. MAC (media access control) layer (IEEE 1609.4) is above the physical layer. MAC layer functionalities are implemented by logical link control (LLC) sublayer (IEEE 802.2) and MAC sublayer (IEEE 802.11P). Network layer (IEEE 1609.3) is the second layer from top and provides different data transmission protocols for VANET communication. The top-most layer is the application layer (IEEE 1609.1); it provides an interaction with hardware devices with required data formatting and interfaces (Figure 2.8).

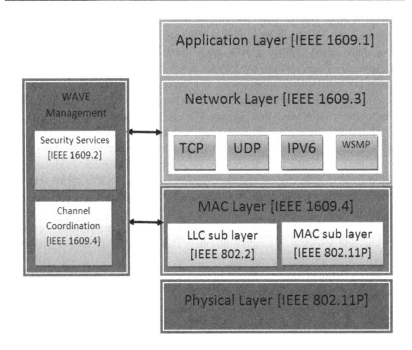

FIGURE 2.8   The IEEE 1609 (WAVE) reference architecture.

2.2.2 IEEE 1609.1 (Network Resources Management)

Its main function is to provide component access to particular processes in the network. This protocol is located in either RSU or OBU. Resource manager (RM) receives requests from applications which are running on different components or computer. Applications that make request to RM are called resource management applications (RMAs). The main function of RMA is to use the resources of OBUs. RM works as a broker between RMAs and OBUs. RM relays commands and responses between RMAs and OBUs. This standard also specifies how the data flows and key features of WAVE system. Command message format and data storage format are decided by this standard.

2.2.3 IEEE 1609.2 (Security Services)

The main goal of IEEE 1609.2 standard is to provide security services in order to avoid malicious user and attacks by them in the vehicular network. Specific message format and message processing steps are specified by this standard. There are authentication of vehicular/RSU nodes in vehicular environments and authentication of different messages in the vehicular network. The IEEE 1609.2 security services are used by security consumers. Security consumers include (1) higher-layer applications and protocols, (2) WAVE provider services that provide services to end users and applications, and (3) WAVE management entities (WMEs) that manage WAVE devices.

The IEEE 1609.2 security services use security data stores (SDSs) to maintain security-related information. Message SDSs are used to store security-related data for each local security consumer on the device. A global SDS is used to store security-related data that are relevant to the entire security services subsystem. The IEEE 1609.2 security services also use the security support services provided by the device on which the security services run. These security support services include providing the current time, current location, and a source of random numbers that the security services need to use to perform security operations.

The functional entities shown in Figure 2.9 access each other's services through service access points (SAPs). Figure 2.9 shows which SAPs related to security services are defined in the current version of IEEE 1609.2. Security services provided by IEEE 1609.2 mainly use elliptic curve cryptography (ECC) algorithms. ECC is public key cryptography that uses public certificates and the public key infrastructure (PKI). There are different entities from the vehicular network.

Certificate Management Entity (CME) manages the certificates that are mentioned as follows:

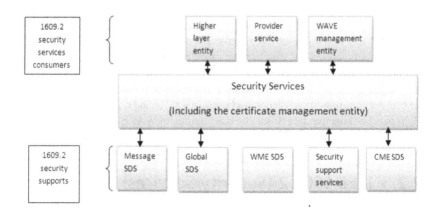

FIGURE 2.9 Security services.

1. CME makes Certificate Revocation List (CRL) certificate request which is made by CA (certificate authority).
2. CME does the processing of certificate, CRL, and other security-related messages.
3. CME keeps track and manages all security-related information.

CME is part of the IEEE 1609.2 security services subsystem. In addition to the certificate management functions provided by the CME, the IEEE 1609.2 security services subsystem also gives cryptographic functionalities like digital signature generation and verification, and encryption or decryption of messages. Security service consumer, such as a vehicle safety application, must obtain a certificate before it can send signed or encrypted messages. Once a certificate is acquired, a security consumer can call the IEEE 1609.2 security services to prepare signed or encrypted messages to send.

2.2.3.1 Certificates and Certificate Authority Hierarchy

Entities that use IEEE 1609.2 security services are classified into two categories: CA entities and end entities. CA entities issue certificates and CRLs. All other entities that use IEEE 1609.2 certificates, but cannot issue certificates or CRLs, are end entities. End entities include vehicles, RSUs, application servers, and applications. The IEEE 1609.2 standard defines the following types of CA entities:

- **Root CAs:** They are trusted to issue certificates to all other CA entities and all end entities. The public keys of a root CA are trusted by end entities, and no certificates for these public keys will be required. A root CA may issue certificates to other CA entities to authorize them to issue certificates or CRLs to end entities.
- **Message CAs:** They issue certificates to end entities that send application messages secured with IEEE 1609.2.
- **WAVE service advertisements (WSA) CAs:** They issue certificates to end entities that send WSA. An end entity uses WSAs to tell other end entities what WAVE services it provides.
- **CRL Signers:** They are CA entities that are authorized to issue CRLs, but cannot issue certificates. The CA hierarchy defined in IEEE 1609.2. IEEE 1609.2 defines three types of end entities: Identified, Identified Not Localized, and WSA Signers. The Identified and the Identified Not Localized end entities are entities that send application messages secured with IEEE 1609.2

security services. These end entities obtain their certificates from the Message CAs. WSA Signers are end entities that send signed WSAs. WSA Signers obtain their certificates from the WSA CAs. All end entities obtain CRLs from the CRL Signer.

The IEEE 1609.2 standard classifies messages into the two basic categories: certificate management messages and application messages. Certificate management messages are the messages sent between end entities (e.g., vehicles) and CA entities to support certificate management functions such as for vehicles to acquire certificates and CRLs from the CA. Application messages are the messages sent by the applications, such as vehicle safety applications, that run on a vehicle or other WAVE devices. Each end entity uses separate sets of certificates to process certificate management messages and application messages. The certificates used to process certificate management messages are called security management certificates. The certificates used to process application messages are called communications certificates. Communication between an end entity and a CA requires a mutual authentication. Mutual authentication process requires two types of security management certificates:

1. A Certificate Signing Request (CSR) certificate used by the end entity to authenticate to the CA
2. A CA certificate used by the CA to authenticate to the end entity. The Identified and the Identified Not Localized end entities use Message CSR certificates to authenticate to the Message CAs. That is, they use Message CSR certificates to sign the Message Certificate Signer Request (CSR) messages they send to the Message CAs to request certificates. The WSA Signers use WSA CSR certificates to authenticate to the WSA CAs.

A certificate contains, implicitly or explicitly, at least one public key for a public key cryptosystem, and a list of the permissions associated with that public key. The permissions specify what the private–public key pair associated with this certificate can be used for.

2.2.3.2 Formats for Public Key, Signature, Certificate, and CRL

This section describes the data structures defined in the IEEE 1609.2 standard for public keys, digital signatures, certificates, and CRLs.

2.2.3.3 Public Key Formats

The IEEE 1609.2 standard uses elliptic curve digital signature algorithm (ECDSA) for digital signatures and elliptic curve integrated encryption scheme (ECIES) for public key encryption. Using ECDSA and ECIES, a public key is a point on an elliptic curve that can be represented by the x- and y-coordinates of this point on the elliptic curve. The IEEE 1609.2 standard defines a public key format, which can be used to encode an ECDSA or ECIES public key. The algorithm field indicates which public key algorithm this public key should be used with. The current IEEE 1609.2 standard supports the following public key algorithms:

- ECDSA over two elliptic curves defined by National Institute of Standards and Technology (NIST) over prime fields: the P244 curve for 112-bit security strength and the P256 curve for 128-bit security strength
- ECIES over the P256 elliptic curve defined by NIST.

2.2.3.4 Certificate Format

The IEEE 1609.2 standard supports both explicit certificates and implicit certificates. An explicit certificate includes the public key certified by the certificate and the digital signature of the certificate issuer. A user verifies the certificate by verifying the certificate issuer's signature. An implicit certificate is a variant of the public key certificate. It does not explicitly include the public key certified by the certificate. Any user can reconstruct the public key from the information on the certificate. An implicit certificate does not include the signature of the certificate issuer. Upon reconstructing the public key, the user simply uses the public key as input to the ECC signature verification algorithm. The signature verification will fail if the certificate is invalid. A main advantage of implicit certificates is that they can be much smaller in size than explicit certificates, making them more efficient for transport over wireless networks.

IEEE 1609.2 gives the certificate format. It consists of three parts:

- A header field called Version-and-Type
- The unsigned certificate in a To-Be-Signed-Certificate format
- The signature of the certificate issuer for explicit certificate or a reconstruction value for reconstructing the public key for an implicit certificate. Certificate explicitly contains the certificate holder's public key and the signature of the CA that issued this certificate.

The CA's signature covers the To-Be-Signed-Certificate. The CA that signed this certificate is identified in the Signer ID field inside the To-Be-Signed-Certificate.

If this is an implicit certificate, it will not explicitly contain the certificate holder's public key or the CA's signature. Instead, it will contain a reconstruction value provided by the CA that can be used by any verifier to recover the certificate holder's public key.

The To-Be-Signed-Certificate contains the certificate contents. This structure has the following main fields:

- The Subject-Type field indicates the type of the certificate. The following types of certificates are defined in the current version of the IEEE 1609.2:
  - Message Anonymous (this field is for future use)
  - Message Identified Not Localized
  - Message Identified Localized
  - Message CSR
  - WSA
  - WSA CSR
  - Message CA
  - WSA CA
  - CRL Signer
  - Root CA.
- The Certificate Content Flag cf indicates whether additional optional fields are present in the certificate.
- The Signer ID field is present only on an explicit certificate, and it will contain the identifier of the certificate of the CA that issued this certificate.
- The identifier of a certificate is the low-order eight octets of the SHA-256 hash value of the certificate.
- The Certificate Specific Data field scope contains information that is unique to this certificate.
- The Expiration field contains the last time the certificate is valid.
- The Lifetime or Start Validity field will be present depending on the value of the Certificate Content Flag. Lifetime means that the certificate is valid from (Expiration − Lifetime) to Expiration. Start Validity means that the certificate is valid from the Start Validity time to the Expiration time.
- The CRL Series field indicates which CRL this certificate will appear on if it is revoked.

- The Verification Key field contains the public key that should be used to verify signatures generated by holder of this certificate. The public key is formatted in the Public Key structure.
- The optional Encryption Key field contains a public key for encryption CRL format.

CRL format consists of three parts:

1. Two header fields
2. The contents of the CRL in the To-Be-Signed CRL format
3. The signature of the CA that issued the CRL.

The first header field version contains the version number of the CRL. Format, which is one in the current version of IEEE 1609.2. The second header field Signer Identifier identifies the certificate for the public key used to generate the signature in the Signature field. This field can contain the following:

- The identifier of the certificate, which is the low-order eight octets of the SHA-256 hash of the certificate
- The certificate itself
- A certificate chain
- The identifier of the certificate and the indication of the public key algorithm when ECDSA is not the public key signature algorithm used to generate the signature in the Signature field.
- The Signature field contains the signature of the CA that issued this CRL, and the signature covers the To-Be-Signed CRL field.

The To-Be-Signed CRL contains information about the revoked certificates and has the following main fields:

- The Type field indicates the type of the entries in the CRL.
- The CRL Series field indicates the CRL series to which this CRL belongs.
- The CA ID field contains the identifier of the CA that issued this CRL.

The identifier of the CA is represented by the low-order eight octets of the hash value of the CA certificate. The CRL Serial field contains the serial number of this CRL. Each time a new CRL is issued; its serial number will increment by one.

- The Start Period and the Issue Date fields define the time period that this CRL covers. That is, this CRL will contain all the certificates belonging to the CRL Series that were revoked within this time period.
- The Next CRL field contains the time when the next CRL is expected to be issued.
- The Certificate Identifiers are the identifiers of the revoked certificates.

The identifier of a revoked certificate is the low-order ten octets of the hash value of the revoked certificate. Optionally, the expiration date of each revoked certificate can also be included.

2.2.4 IEEE 802.11P (Physical Layer)

Physical layer is the bottommost layer from WAVE architecture, and it is very similar to OSI model seventh layer. It provides a link between the MAC layer and the medium used for sending and transmitting data block. It is responsible for data formatting according to network requirements.

This layer consists of two layers [5,6]:

1. **Physical Layer Convergence Protocol (PLCP):** This protocol is responsible for communication with MAC layer and transforms data packet coming from MAC layer to OFDM frame.
2. **Physical Medium Access (PMD):** It is a link between the physical transmission medium and fiber links.

Physical layer in DSRC is a modification in the existing IEEE standards to satisfy the vehicular network requirement. Challenges faced by the vehicular network are collision avoidance between vehicles, message formatting speed, and low latency requirement. IEEE 802.11P, i.e., DSRC for VANET, states the latency of 50–100 ms. It improves the performance of physical layer and gives robust, scalable, and low latency in communication. Low latency avoids accidents and saves life in the vehicular environment. It also achieves a minimum bit error rate. Basic technical factors in communication like encoding, modulation, and unutilized subcarrier affect the performance of physical layer. Physical layer in VANET is critical and responsible for providing better performance of network.

2.2.5 IEEE 802.11P (MAC Layer)

MAC layer is present between data link layer and physical layer in OSI model. It provides easy control to the nodes for communication. MAC layer in IEEE 802.11p plays an important role in faster and efficient communication.

In VANET, vehicles and RSU transmit different messages. Messages are mainly classified as safety and nonsafety messages. Single channel is used to transmit all these messages, which make it difficult to guarantee quality of service. It may cause congestions in network due to less important messages and avoid important/emergency messages from transmitting. Safety messages in VANET play an important role in avoiding accidents, traffic jam situation, and other on-road situations. Performance of vehicular network will be affected due to single-channel use for different messages. As multiple users can access channel at the same time, there are chances of attack on messages. Solution to resolve the problem of safety and effective transmission of messages is multichannel MAC. Multichannel MAC facilitates nodes with different channels to communicate with each other. It makes access more easy and flexible. Vehicular network with multichannel MAC achieve better performance in the form of throughput and less delay than a single-channel network [7–10].

2.2.6 IEEE 1609.3 (Networking Services)

IEEE 1609.3 standard protocol is used to provide network services. It consists of two services: data plane and management plane services. Service includes two devices, namely, provider device that sends WSA messages to indicate its availability for use services of SCHs. Provider device is WSA service initiator; and user device that monitors the received WSAs. As per the availability of SCH channel, user device receives WSA and joins the service [11,12].

2.2.6.1 Data Plane Services

Data plane network services support two protocol stacks: WSMP and IPv6 protocol stacks.

1. **WAVE Short Message Protocol (WSMP):** WAVE Short Message Protocol (WSMP) is used to achieve time-efficient and priority-based message transmission. It is a WAVE network-layer unique protocol. When WAVE short message data units are received from upper layers, WSMP generates WSMP header and is added to receive unit, and makes packet transmission request to LLC.

LLC sets the ether type field value to encapsulate the packet and pass the data to the lower layers. When the LLC receives MAC data unit, it checks the ether type field value, then delivers it to either IPv6 or WSMP stack [11,12].

2. **Internet Protocol Version 6 IPv6:** WAVE standards support User Datagram Protocol (UDP) or Transmission Control Protocol or Internet Protocol. LLC sublayers are utilized to send and receive IP traffic.

2.2.6.2 Management Plane Services

- **WAVE Management Entity (WME):** WME provides network management services to WAVE. It serves all service request of higher layers and channel assignments; monitors WAVE Service Announcements (WSA); configures IPv6 using data received from other WAVE devices; and maintains Management Information Base (MIB).

- **Management Information Base (MIB):** MIB provides a channel-related information like all transmitter details in tabular form with their available timing info. It also has system configuration and system status information. Number of channels supported, advertiser identity, registration port, and WMS maximum length are part of system configuration information. Group of status tables, namely, Provider Service Request Table (PSRT), User Service Request Table (USRT), CCH Service Request Table (CSRT), and WSM Service Request Table (WSRT), is part of system status information. PSRT is table located in MIB and maintains provider information such as Provider Service Identifier (PSID) of the registered application, IPv6 address, port number, and so on. MIB consists of USRT for maintaining information such as user PSIDs, advertiser identifier, link quality, channel number, and so on; CSRT is responsible to manage CCH interval, request priority, and request status; and WSRT consists of PSIDs of the registered applications [11,12].

- **WAVE Services Request:** WAVE service requests are of six types. It mainly includes services of adding, updating, and deleting. WME accepts the provider service requests which are generated by higher-layer entity and assigns the SCH access. It also triggers the MLME to start generating WSAs.

- **User Service Request:** User service request is made by higher layer, when WME broadcasting for WSAs. If required SCH is available, it assigns SCH access. When a higher layer generates a WSM service request and shows an interest to receive WSM of a particular PSID, the WME accepts the request and ongoing of its monitoring; it delivers any received WSMs with matching PSID to the requested higher entity.

- **CCH Service Request:** Whenever a higher layer requires ongoing CCH access during a particular interval for a WSM activity or WSA reception, CCH service request is generated, which will be considered by WME.
- **Management Data Service Request:** WME accepts all the request of management data entity for vendor-specific action (VSA) frames. It assigns SCH to serve request and trigger the MLME to generate VSA frame.
- **Timing Advertisement Service Request:** WME accepts the request from management data entity for timer advertisement service request and transmits TA frame. WME assigns SCH or CCH and triggers the MLME to generate the TA frame [11,12].
- **WSM Frame Format:** Data structure used to send WAVE short messages is called as WSM frame. This frame consists of different fields, namely, version field WSMP which shows the version of the WAVE protocol, Provider Service Identifier field (PSID), Channel Number field which defines the channel that is used for communication, Data Rate field which specifies the data rate used in transmission, WAVE element ID field which represents WSMP header, WAVE Length field which determines length of the data field, and WSM Data field which contains the payload data, e.g., "Hello World."
- **WSA Frame Format:** Availability of service is announced by provider by sending WSA frame. This frame is also a data structure like other frames.

2.2.7 IEEE 1609.4 (Multichannel Operations)

Basic IEEE 802.11 is extended to this standard. It gives multichannel services to the vehicular environment. This standard is making possible to manage coordination of channel selection and maximum utilization of available spectrum. It avoids congestion and also makes available separate channel of highest-priority messages.

Multichannel operations under IEEE 1609.4 standard in VANETs define a number of channels. Every channel has distinct applications and distinct characteristics, as shown in Figure 2.10. As shown in diagram, every channel not only uses distinct frequencies but also has different transmission powers.

Channel Number	172	174	176	178	180	182	184
Channel Type	Service Channel	Service Channel	Service Channel	Control Channel	Service Channel	Service Channel	Service Channel
Application	Non-Safety	Non-Safety	Traffic Efficiency	Critical Safety	Critical Safety	Traffic Efficiency	Traffic Efficiency
Radio Range	V2V	Medium	Medium	All	Short	Short	Intersection
Tx Power Level	33 dBm	33 dBm	33 dBm	44.8 dBm	23 dBm	23 dBm	40 dBm
	5.855	5.865	5.875	5.885	5.895	5.905	5.915	5.925

FIGURE 2.10   A set of channels for multichannel operations in WAVE.

Channel used for safety-critical control messages has the highest potential transmission power, while channel used for noncritical control messages has less-priority applications and short-range safety.

Applications are provided/use channels with smaller allowed transmit powers. IEEE 1609.4 time multiplex division method is used to determine SCH and CCH. Every alternate time slot is given to CCH. SCH utilizes the remaining time slot as per the system requirement. The IEEE 1609.4 multi-channel operation is implemented with priority scheme in IEEE 802.11p MAC layer. It is very similar to the IEEE 802.11e. Channel has four access categories, denoted by AC0–AC3. AC3 has the highest priority among these categories. For the plain enhanced distributed coordination function (EDCA), frames with different data contents get placed in different queues. Internal contention procedure is applied to serve these contents, as shown in Figure 2.11.

Different channel and different access categories' queues have different timer settings related to the internal contention procedure.

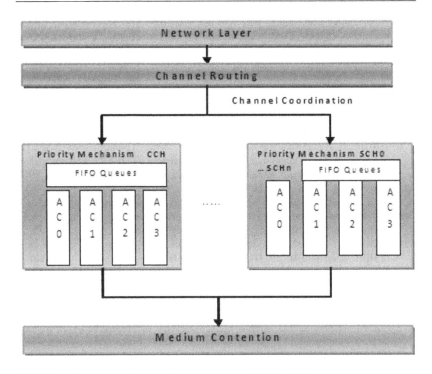

FIGURE 2.11   Internal contention process for 802.11pMAC.

REFERENCES

1. S. P. Godse and P. N. Mahalle, "Intelligent authentication and message forwarding in VANET". *International Journal of Smart Vehicles and Smart Transportation (IJSVST)*, vol. 3, no. 1, pp. 1–20, 2020. doi:10.4018/IJSVST.2020010101.
2. F. D. da Cunha, L. Villas, et al., "Data communication in VANETs: Survey, applications and challenges", *Ad-Hoc Networks*, vol. 44, pp. 90–103, 2016. Elsevier.
3. E. C. Eze, S.-J. Zhang, E.-J. Liu, and J. C. Eze, "Advances in vehicular ad-hoc networks (VANETs): Challenges and road-map for future development", *International Journal of Automation and Computing*, vol. 13, no. 1, pp. 1–18, February 2016.
4. S. Godse and P. Mahalle, "Rising issues in VANET communication and security: A state of art survey", *International Journal of Advanced Computer Science and Applications (IJACSA)*, vol. 8, no. 9, pp. 245–252, 2017.

5. A.M.S. Abdelgader and L. Wu, "The physical layer of the IEEE 802.11p WAVE communication standard: The specifications and challenges", *Proceedings of the World Congress on Engineering and Computer Science 2014 Vol II WCECS 2014*, San Francisco, USA, 22–24 October, 2014.

6. P. Van Wijngaarden, Frame capture in IEEE 802.s11p vehicular networks, a simulation-based approach. Faculty of Electrical Engineering, Mathematics and Computer Science.

7. K. Bilstrup, E. Uhlemann, E. G. Ström, and U. Bilstrup, "Evaluation of the IEEE 802.11p MAC method for Vehicle-to-Vehicle Communication".

8. J. Misic, G. Badawy, S. Rashwand, and V. B. Misic, "Tradeoff issues for CCH/SCH duty cycle for IEEE 802.11p single channel devices", *IEEE Communications Society Subject Matter Experts for Publication in the IEEE Globecom 2010 Proceedings*, Miami, Florida, USA.

9. IEEE Std. 802.11e-2005, Part 11: Wireless LAN Medium Access Control (MAC) and Physical Layer (PHY) Specifications: Amendment 8: Medium Access Control (MAC) Quality of Service Enhancements, 2005.

10. L. Miao, K. Djouani, B. J. Van Wyk, and Y. Hamam, "Performance evaluation of IEEE 802.11p MAC PROTOCOl in VANETs safety applications", *2013 IEEE Wireless Communications and Networking Conference (WCNC): Networks*, Shanghai, China.

11. 1609.3-2010- IEEE Standard for Wireless Access in Vehicular Environments (WAVE) - Networking Services, 1–144.

12. S.A. M. Ahmed, S. H. S. Ariffin, et al., "Overview of wireless access in vehicular environment (WAVE) protocols and standards", *Indian Journal of Science and Technology*, vol. 6, no. 7, pp. 1–8, July 2013.

Message Forwarding Strategies in VANET

3

3.1 INTRODUCTION

The main goal of establishing any network is to share/pass different information among nodes in the network. The first step in communication is to make available channels/routes for communication between the source and the destination. Once route is selected for communication, data is forward on that path. For selecting an effective route, various routing algorithms are available. In any network, messages that are used to establish a network and to manage the network are known as control messages. Once the network is established, participants start using services of the network. They can transfer their own messages to desired recipients. These messages are also called as service messages. VANET (vehicular ad hoc network) is used for intelligent transportation system. Messages in VANET address different services on road, which make safe, fast, and comfort in transportation with a minimum use of human resources. This chapter will give an introduction to service messages and strategies of message forwarding.

3.2 TYPES OF MESSAGES IN VANET

VANET messages are categorized into two types: service messages and control messages, as shown in Figure 3.1.

Service-oriented messages are further classified into safety messages (contain emergency messages) and nonsafety messages (lesser-priority messages that mainly point to multimedia data (audio/video) or other lesser-priority information). Control messages can be categorized into three types: network setup messages (messages are used for the initial network setup), authentication messages (messages are responsible for authentication and detection of malicious nodes), and network policy update messages (messages guide about different policies of network usages).

3.1.1 Service Messages

Messages that are used to request different services and provide reply to that request are referred as service-based messages. These messages are of two types: safety and nonsafety messages.

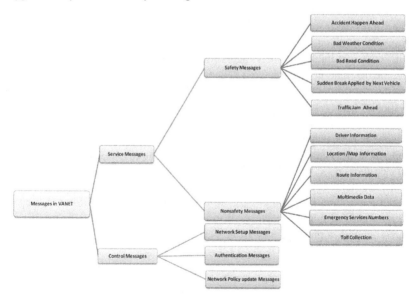

FIGURE 3.1 Classifications of messages in VANET.

3.1.1.1 Safety Messages

Messages give different alerts when vehicles are moving on road. These messages provide information about how to avoid accidents, traffic jam situation, and some time-consuming traveling situation. Safety messages directly help the driver to save time by avoiding traffic jam roads or to save life of traveler by avoiding accidents on road. Messages under this category are at the highest priority than other messages. Let's see each message under this category. Here, we considered essential messages, but it may not be sufficient; new messages can be added as per the requirements and emergencies in a particular country, state, or city.

- **Accident happens ahead:** If accident happens on road, it should be informed to other vehicles which are on the same path. Vehicles that reach at this location sense the accident event and generate an accident message. This vehicle broadcasts the message to all neighboring vehicles. It helps to avoid further accident because of the already-happened accident. It also avoids traffic jam situation by diverting other vehicles' route to different roads.
- **Bad weather condition:** Bad weather can become a reason for accidents and traffic jams. People can be caught into trouble due to bad weather. Heavy rain, high winds, wildfires, heavy snow falls, tropical cyclones, fogs, etc. are bad weather situations. In history, there are many losses to transport networks and lives caused by these bad weather situations. If the driver receives an alert about bad weather before he enters into those regions, then it will save lives and reduce wastage of time. These messages will be broadcasted by regional RSU (road side unit) to other RSUs in order to alert all vehicles in their range.
- **Bad road condition:** Road conditions play an important role in safe, comfortable, and in-time journey. They also avoid accidents and damage of vehicles. RSUs make available this information to users. As per the road condition, the user can decide the road selection.
- **Sudden break applied by the next vehicle:** This is one of the reasons for accident occurring all over the world. The reason behind the sudden break applied may be an obstacle in the way of vehicle. The obstacle can be an animal, tree, human being, path hole, etc. Due to the sudden break applied by the vehicle, the driver of the vehicle that follows behind does not get sufficient time to take decision of applying break, and thus, the vehicle behind crashes with

the vehicle that applied break. If an alert message will be delivered while break is applied by the vehicle, it will make the driver of the vehicle that follows behind to apply break and thus avoid the accident.

- **Traffic jam condition:** Most of the time the reason for traffic jam is that we do not have traffic updates of particular regions. If we get a traffic jam alert priorly, it will help the driver to select less traffic path. It will avoid extra traffic jam on the same road. It will distribute the vehicles on different parallel roads for the same destination. It saves time and achieves an effective utilization of the road network.

3.1.1.2 Nonsafety Messages

These messages make driving comfortable and easy by providing additional information about roads and any requested data. These types of messages are having less priority as compared to alert messages but important in considering time saving and driver's comfort. Let's see each message under this category:

- **Driver information:** One vehicle can make request for driver information to other vehicle for specific purpose. Driver information is normally kept secret, but in some emergency cases, it is required. RSU may require driver information if any driver is breaking traffic rules.
- **Location map information:** While driving a vehicle, driver may not be aware with the path to reach at destination. He can make a request for a map for particular location. Vehicle driver can use the map for navigation. It will save time and avoid confusion of driver.
- **Routing path information:** It is a part of navigation facility. A vehicle's driver can make a request for route by giving source and destination to another vehicle or RSU. Routing facility can suggest the shortest path between the source and the destination. It can also provide an alternative path to the current path used by the driver. It can give the shortest path to visit more than two locations in the same trip. It depends on user's requirement, i.e., what he exactly wants. It makes driver comfortable for driving in new regions.
- **Request for multimedia data:** If a vehicle driver wants some multimedia data like songs, movies, data/information about any entity, he can broadcast a request for the same. Multimedia data makes traveler trip comfortable.

- **Toll collection:** These messages provide information about toll plaza ahead and its charges as per vehicle type. Vehicle identification and deduction of toll amount from the user account (which is connected with the toll system) take place. Vehicles will get toll receipts with amount and necessary details of journey.
- **Emergency services number:** On express highway or highway, the user may be caught in emergency situations like accident, robbery, and vehicle breakdowns on road, medical emergency due to accident, or health issues. All these emergencies require the respective assistant to provide the required help on road. User will be provided with police, hospital, crane, garages, etc. The nearest available locations and contact numbers of the respective services are made available to users.

3.1.2 Control Messages

These messages are used to control the network-related operations. Network activities are mainly categorized in to three types: the initial network setup, security of network, and deciding and monitoring network policy.

- **Network setup messages:** These messages are used for the initial setup activities of the network. In a vehicular network, nodes are nothing but vehicles and RSUs. A registration of vehicles and RSUs with a trusted authority is the first step in the network setup. Clock synchronization, hello messages, beaconing, and sharing credential by higher authorities are some initial messages used to establish the network.
- **Authentication messages:** Once registration and setup process are completed, whenever a vehicle enters into a new region of RSU, authentication of that vehicle is done by the RSU. These messages involve sharing of certificates and keys by one vehicle with the RSU or another vehicle. Prevention and detection of malicious nodes takes place by using these messages. Misbehavior of nodes is notified to other vehicles by the blacklist published at a specific time period.
- **Network policy update messages:** Policy/rules of usages of network are updated from time to time. These updated policies are conveyed to the user through policy messages. They also keep control/watch on policy disobey by user. Users that disobey policies are warned or punished by admin controller.

3.3 MESSAGE FORWARDING STRATEGIES

3.3.1 Basic Strategies for Message Forwarding in Network

Forwarding messages, i.e., data or information, is an important aspect of any network. Unicast, broadcast, multicast, and geocast are some important types of message forwarding [1].

- **Unicasting:** In this type of communication, one node communicates with one particular node from the network. The sender node attaches the address of the receiver node while transmitting messages (Figure 3.2).

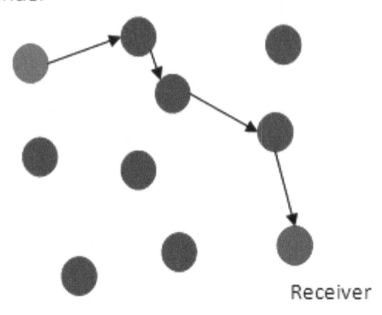

FIGURE 3.2 Unicasting.

- **Multicasting:** In this type of communication, the sender node sends messages to multiple nodes in the network. The sender node forwards the same message to multiple nodes. It provides the address of multiple nodes while transmitting message (Figure 3.3).
- **Broadcasting:** In this type of message, the forwarding sender node broadcasts the message to all nodes in the network. The sender node broadcasts the message into the network, which is received by neighboring nodes that are involved in further broadcasting process. This process will continue still each node in the network receives the message (Figure 3.4).
- **Geocasting:** This is a special type of broadcasting where sender node forwards message to all nodes in a particular geographical location (Figure 3.5).

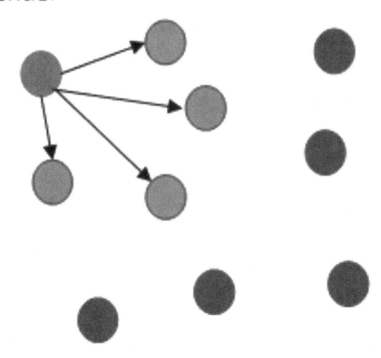

Sender

FIGURE 3.3 Multicasting.

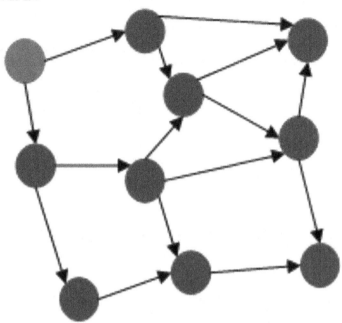

FIGURE 3.4 Broadcasting.

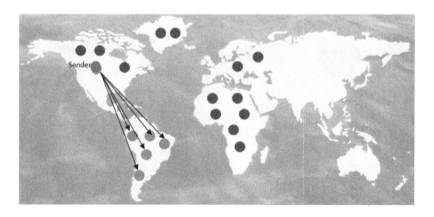

FIGURE 3.5 Geocasting.

These are basic message forwarding schemes in the network, which are further modified by different researchers as per domain and their communication requirements. In VANET, the speed of nodes (vehicles) is very high. It makes the network very dynamic. Due to dynamic nature and directional issues of vehicles (vehicles may travel opposite to one another), it is a volatile network and needs to satisfy the special requirements for establishing communication.

3.3.2 Requirements of VANET for Message Forwarding

- **Speed:**
- **Bandwidth:** 1–40 MHz
- **Communication frequencies:** It uses frequencies ranging from 5.8 to 5.9 GHz.
- **Latency:** VANET requires low latency for effective communication.
- **Routing protocol:** It depends on the type of communication.

3.3.3 Challenges in VANET Message Forwarding

- **Speed of message forwarding:** As messages in VANET are very sensitive and life critical, there is a need of timely dissemination of message at the respective destination node. Speed of messages is dependent on channel bandwidth, availability of channel, selected route etc. [2].
- **Categorization of messages as per their importance:** It is necessary to categorize messages as per their type. Messages in VANET are mainly divided into two types: safety and nonsafety messages. Before assigning priority to messages, they are classified into these two types.
- **Sequence of messages dissemination:** After the classification of messages, priority is assigned to each and every message as per their severity. Sequence of message dissemination is decided based on their priorities. Assigning priorities to messages at the node level is a challenging task.

3.3.4 Message Forwarding Strategies in VANET Used by Previous Researchers

- **Flooding:** [3] It is a way to communicate message in the network. In this strategy, the vehicle sends information or messages to neighboring nodes. Receiver nodes send the same information to next nodes. This process is continuing until all vehicles receive the same information. This scheme is better for a sparse network where nodes are scattered and less in number. In high-density network, it faces collisions, contention, and message redundancy problem.
- **Probabilistic scheme:** [4,5] It broadcasts messages with some fixed probability; it avoids collision, contention, and redundant messages in the network. The probability of receiving the same packet is less in sparse network. It works like flooding in case the probability is increased [7]. In dense network, this scheme gives high performance. In low-density/sparse network, the performance is low.
- **Counter-based technique:** This scheme sets counter for each message [6,7]. If the same message is received repeatedly, the counter gets incremented by one. If the counter value of the redundant message is less than the threshold value, then the packet will be forwarded; otherwise, the packet is discarded.
- **Distance-based scheme:** [7,8] It considers distance of neighboring nodes. If nodes are at threshold distances, then the message is forwarded by the sender; otherwise, it ignores the message.
- **Location-based scheme:** [5,7,9] It first measures the coverage area with the help of sender location. Packet is ignored by the vehicle if it is received from the node in smaller area than the threshold; otherwise, the packet will be broadcasted.
- **Neighbor knowledge methods:** [5,10] In this method, a table is maintained for storing information of neighboring nodes. A vehicle will take decision of forwarding and retaining packets based on information available in the table. To obtain neighboring node information, each vehicle shares hello packets with their neighbors to get current information. Received information is stored in their table for future by each vehicle. This method totally relies on the exchange of hello packet. If the interval between vehicles is short, contention and collision will happen, and if the interval is large, then it degrades the performance of network due to mobility.
- **Relevance-based approach:** In this approach, the relevance of message is decided. If message is relevant and important, only then it is forwarded to the next node. As low-priority messages are discarded

from sending, it saves time [11]. Relevance of messages is decided by vehicle context, message context, and information context.

*   **An adaptive broadcast protocol:** Two important challenges in message forwarding are the existence of no priority mechanism and the existence of hidden node. An adaptive broadcast protocol is designed with the aim of reliable broadcasting. Each packet is assigned with a sequence number, which helps to analyze the congestion of network. Vehicles adjust the contention window with reference to sequence number and improve the performance [12].

3.4 MESSAGE PACKET FORMAT

As we have seen, messages in VANET are categorized into different types. These messages are forwarded as per the situation or requirements from one vehicle to another vehicles or RSU. While preparing messages for transmission, a standard packet format is designed by researcher as per their requirements. Here, event/message packet contains event type, event location, event timestamp, trust value (TV) of event, and reputation value (RV) of event.

EVENT TYPE	EVENT TIME	EVENT LOCATION	EVENT TRUST VALUE	EVENT REPUTATION VALUE
Type(E)	$T(E)$	$L(E)$	$TV(E)$	$RV(E)$

Message/event is generated or sensed by node. Every event is generated with a packet format as mentioned above. Node broadcasts this event to the neighboring nodes. Neighboring node first validates the source of event by using local certificate of source node. After that, it validates the message forwarded by the source node. Message integrity or originality is validated using a hash function.

3.5 NEED OF PRIORITY-BASED MESSAGE FORWARDING

As we have seen, vehicles in the network can pass different types of messages in the network. This message may be from safety and nonsafety types of services. It may be from control messages to set up network or to find the routing path.

It is necessary to reach important messages first to their destination. If vehicles receive different messages at a time from the network, then there should be mechanism which can decide which message should be forwarded first as per emergency or importance. Forwarding messages without priority will make network busy with transmission of less important messages. VANET is a real-time network where message delivery in time is very important. It may cause traffic jam situation or accident on road. Priority-based message forwarding mechanism will improve the performance of transportation system and maximize the utilization of the vehicular network. Classifying messages into different types and assigning priorities to messages as per category are challenging tasks.

3.5.1 Survey of Priority-Based Messages Schemes by Previous Researchers

Different safety messages are assigned with the respective priority in a VANET. The vehicular network has the following *aspects*: (1) due to high-speed vehicular nodes, it has high bit error rate; (2) vehicles running in the same direction are using road topology. Relative velocity of vehicle running in the same direction is low; and (3) safety messages used in the communication network are assigned with priority. High-priority messages are mostly transmitted instead of low-priority messages, which saves the number of bits transmission to transmit low-priority messages [13].

Mobility-centric data dissemination algorithm for vehicular networks (MDDV) treats high-density and low-density regions separately. Messages are transmitted as per geographical density. As there is no end-to-end connectivity between vehicles, intermediate vehicles play a role of router and disseminate messages opportunistically. Opportunistic message transmission algorithm answers the questions about who can send, when to send, and when to store/drop messages. Using a generic mobile computing approach, vehicles perform local operations based on their own knowledge while their collective behavior achieves a global objective [14].

Priority-based message delivery approach in VANET is suggested for time-sensitive traffic in VANET. In this approach, priority-based message scheduling technique with backoff mechanism is introduced. Priority calculation function is assigning priority to messages, and messages as per priority are transmitted from the node [15].

In this scheme, the researcher made a classification of vehicles into three categories: emergency vehicle, registered vehicle, and unregistered vehicle. Vehicle movements are monitored by control center. Emergency vehicles are given the highest priority for movement. Medium priority is given to registered vehicle. Unregistered vehicles are at low priority. Chord algorithm is implemented to avoid accidents; it is also used to control the speed of the vehicle. Vehicles' speed is monitored and controlled by the chord algorithm to prevent accidents [12].

The author comes up with advanced navigation scheme which guides the driver for reaching destination in time. This approach uses the real-time traffic information in a distributed manner and provides it to the vehicle driver. An algorithm is developed for getting a real-time data of traffic conditions, congestion caused by different emergency event on road, and providing proper guidance to the user. The algorithm assures that data provided is based on the context of driver. Identity of driver is kept secure by anonymous user strategy. Process delay parameter is used to evaluate the scheme [16].

This scheme uses beaconing with safety beacon term for data transmission. The data with these additional features helps to improve routing speed and security. Factors considered in this scheme are the size of beacon frames and reception count. Increase in size of beacon increases the performance of all parameters. The author also proposed a mathematical model along with Proof of Concept [17].

The author provides a solution for issues in VANET with Bluetooth Low Energy (BLE). This scheme also uses Wi-Fi in V2V communication. The result of this scheme shows that minimum latency and required distance between two moving objects can be achieved by using this scheme. Establishing trust between vehicles is also considered in this method of communication [18].

Scheme in this research paper uses TV to categorize messages. It uses the hybrid approaches which make use of pros of role-based trust and experience-based trust. It also uses data mining concepts for decision-making [19].

Scheme in this paper explains security issues in V2V communication. It makes decision for accepting and rejecting messages based on safety analysis. It uses a Certificate Revocation List for analysis. It defines a model for detecting confidence on security (CoS) infrastructure of VANET. CoS can take a decision of accepting or rejecting messages at each node level in V2V communication [20].

Literature survey comes with the conclusion that some scheme has problems in end-to-end connectivity. Few scheme fails in low density due to frequent retransmittance of packets. Many schemes cause an issue of collision in high-density network. Few schemes categorize vehicles as unregistered and registered vehicles, and assign low priority to unregistered vehicles. Every time applying vehicle traffic flow theory to transmit packets is time-consuming. Some schemes consider high-, medium-, and low-density vehicular network separately. There is a need of better priority-based message forwarding scheme, which can consider all above limitations.

3.6 PROPOSED PRIORITY ASSIGNING MECHANISM [21]

1. **Objective 1:** Priority-based message forwarding in VANET for effective communication and navigation.
2. **Objective 2:** Intelligent message forwarding in VANET when the first event is sensed by the vehicle. Consider that an event sensed by the vehicle is an accident on road. Vehicle passing from accident location and the vehicle involved in accident both pass the event information to the neighboring vehicles. Receiving vehicles perform the following steps before taking decision on message forwarding.
   - Authenticate source node using its local certificate.
   - Validate message by its RV.
   - Check the integrity of message by hash function.
   - Detect Sybil and replay attack by verifying location and time stamp.

Two-point checking system is applied by the receiver node: first is TV checking, and the second is RV checking. Every node maintains a list of all nodes IP (Internet Protocol). If event message is received, it marks the value of sender IP in the list as 1, and RV of sender node is added to RV value of receiver node. If message comes repeatedly from the same nodes, then the receiver node TV will not change, but RV will change. If maximum numbers of time nodes sense the event, then it shows that the message is genuine. Before forwarding message to the next node, the receiver node checks the validity of sender nodes by its local certificate. For priority-based message forwarding, priority of different types of events is decided by setting different threshold values of TV and RV. Messages/events in VANET are classified into two types: safety messages and nonsafety messages. Safety messages include messages like accident, bad weather, sudden break applied by the next vehicle, and traffic jam situation. Nonsafety messages include data/information like location/map information, driver information, routing path information, and request for multimedia data. TV and RV threshold values with respect to type of messages are shown in Table 3.1. If TV and RV reach their threshold limit, then the type of message/event is forwarded by the node to the next node. Another precaution taken to avoid a delay in message forwarding is that after a certain time interval, RV value starts decreasing by 1. So, even if messages come faster from other nodes, it is immediately forwarded; otherwise, it is discarded.

TABLE 3.1 TV and RV threshold values for message forwarding

SR NO	MESSAGE TYPE	$TV_{THRESHOLD}$ VALUE	$RV_{THRESHOLD}$ VALUE
1	Accident	2	5
2	Sudden break applied	4	10
3	Bad weather	6	15
4	Traffic jam	8	20
5	Driver information	10	25
6	Location or map information	12	30
7	Routing path information	14	35
8	Request for multimedia data	16	40

Event Packet Type: [Message, Event_location, Trust value, Reputation value, Type (Event)]

$$\mathbf{IMF(E, N)} = \int_{v=0}^{N} \left(\text{Auth}(t) - \sum_{i}^{TV} \text{Sense}_{\text{type}}(E) + \sum_{i}^{RV} |v| \right) dT, \qquad (3.1)$$

where

IMF means intelligent message forwarding.

Whenever a node gets the event, first it authenticates the source node, and if that node is valid, it starts to assign RV and TV for every node and event. And depending on the TV and RV, node decides whether this event should be forwarded or not. If yes, then it decides the interval of time as well.

Step 1: Detect/Generate Event

$M = L(E), T(E), \text{Type}(E), \ \text{TV}(E), \text{RV}(E),$

    where

        L(E)=location of event, **T(E)**=time of event/event time stamp, **Type(E)**=type of event, **TV(E)**=trust value (for checking vehicle trust), and **RV(E)**=reputation value (for checking message sense).

        Start

        Generate Event Message 'M'.

        HM=Hash (M).

        End

Step 2: Authentication:
Authentication of nodes is considered by new enhanced ECC (elliptic curve cryptography) scheme which we implemented. Steps of ECC algorithm are as given below.

A: Initialization phase

- **TA (Trusted authority):**
  1. TA shares unique ID (PID_i), secret key (SK_i), hash function (HF), and prime secret key of TA, i.e., "s" to all vehicles.
  2. TA shares secret key (SK_r) and certificate to all RSUs.
  3. Key is periodically changed.
- **RSU (Road side unit):**
  1. RSU keeps the record of the last time stamp of each vehicle in its range from start timing of simulator to ending time of simulator.
  2. RSU also keeps the record of the last three locations of each vehicle in its range.
- **Vehicle:**
  1. Receives TA initial data.
  2. Each vehicle keeps counter for RV and TV.
  3. Calculates its public key (PK_i) from secret key (SK_i).
  4. Applies hash function.

$$TA \begin{cases} \text{share(uniqueID, Secret Key, HashFunction, s) to all Vehicles} \\ \text{Share (Secret key, Certificate) to All RSU} \\ \text{Periodic Change (ECC Key)} \end{cases}$$

$$RSU \begin{cases} \int_{start}^{end} \text{Vehicle}(V_i) \rightarrow \text{Last TimeStamp} \\ \int_{start}^{end} \text{Vehicle}(V_i) \rightarrow \langle \text{Location1} | \text{Location2} | \text{Location3} \rangle \end{cases}$$

$$Vehicle \begin{cases} TA_{Initial} Data(.) \\ \text{ReputationValue} - RV \\ \text{Trusted Value} - TV \\ PK_i = Sk_i.P \bmod n \\ PID_i = Hash(Pk_i \parallel s) \end{cases}$$

B: Certificate generation:

In this phase, local certificate is generated and assigned to vehicles by RSU. Process of certificate generation is initiated when any new vehicle makes a request to RSU for communication. In detail, process of certificate generation is explained with steps and Figure 3.6 of sequence diagram.

Step 1: ith vehicle makes a request for local certificate to RSU_r. It forwards its own public key PK_i and identity PID_i to RSU_r.

Step 2: RSU_r forwards public key (PK_i) and identity (PID_i) of vehicle to trusted authority for validation.

Step 3: Trusted authority server verifies PK_i and PID_i in database. If it is present, then it declares vehicle as valid/authentic vehicle.

Step 4: After the validation of vehicle, RSU_r initiates the process of certificate generation.

Step 5: Local certificate is generated by RSU_r

$PKr = skr \cdot P \bmod n$ (1) // Public key of RSU_r

$SKri = PKr \oplus PKi \bmod n$ (2) // Session key from RSU to vehicle

$HVri = hash(P\,IDi \parallel Certr)$ (3) // Hash value from RSU to vehicle

$Lcertri = HVri \times SKri \bmod n$ (4) // Local certificate from RSU to vehicle

$CL\_List[P\,IDi, SKri, Lcertri, T]$ // Certification list at RSU side stores local certificate, identity of vehicle, and time slot for which certificate is valid

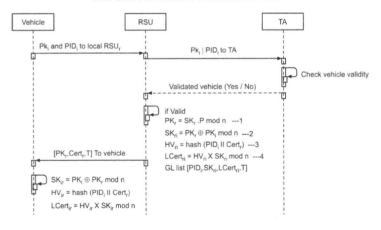

FIGURE 3.6 Local certificate generation at RSU side.

Step 6: [*PKr*, *Certr*, *T*] *To Vehicle* // RSU sends its own public key, certificate, and time slot to vehicle

Step 7: Local certificate (LCert$_{ir}$) for vehicle-to-RSU communication is generated using the following steps:

SKir = *PKi* ⊕ *PKr* **mod** *n* // Session key from vehicle to RSU

HVir = *hash*(*P IDi* ∥ *Certr*) // Hash value from vehicle to RSU

Lcertir = *HVir* × *SKir* **mod** *n* // Local certificate for vehicle to RSU

Authentication of vehicle by RSU is explained in detail with sequence diagram.

Step 1: Vehicle "*i*" sends original message (*M*), message hash value (HM$_i$), its own identity (PID$_i$), and local certificate encrypted using session key from vehicle to RSU (SK$_{ir}$).

Step 2: Vehicle "*j*" sends encrypted local certificate to RSU. RSU decrypts it with session key from RSU to vehicle (SK$_{ri}$).

Step 3: RSU compares the received local certificate with stored certificate in CL. If it is present, vehicle is authenticated else it will not authenticated.

Step 4: Vehicle "*j*" applies a hash function on original message received from vehicle "*i*" if HM$_i$=HM$_j$. Message is valid (Figure 3.7).

C: Event generation/detection and forwarding

Vehicles may generate their own event or detect the event generated by some other vehicles. After event generation or detection, it is forwarded by vehicle considering node validation and message validation. In detail, steps of vehicle authentication and message validations are explained in Figure 3.8.

– Detect/generate event

$$M = L(E), T(E), \text{Type}(E), \text{RV}(E), \text{TV}(E)$$

$$HM = \text{Hash}(M)$$

where

$L(E)$=location of event.
$T(E)$=*time* of event.
Type(E)=type of event

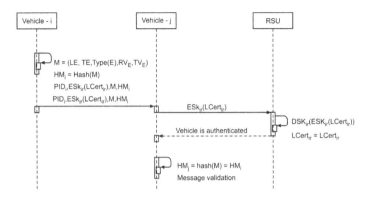

FIGURE 3.7   Vehicle and message validation.

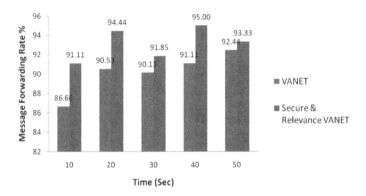

FIGURE 3.8   Message forwarding rate with respect to time.

$RV(E)$ = reputation value of event.
$TV(E)$ = trust value of event.

Step 3: Forward event to NN (neighboring nodes)
  Event management

$$RV(E) = \int_{vi}^{vnn} \sum \text{Event Sense dnn}, \tag{3.2}$$

where (V_{nn} = total number of neighboring nodes)

$$TV(E) = \int_{vi}^{vnn} \text{calc(Value) dnn} \tag{3.3}$$

$$\text{Calc(Value)} = \begin{cases} \text{if } vi \ \text{ sense event,} & \text{then value} = 1 \\ \text{if } vi \ \text{ not sense event,} & \text{then value} = 0 \end{cases}$$

$$\text{If} \left(\text{TV} = \text{TV}_{\text{Threshold}} \ \&\& \ \text{RV} = \text{RV}_{\text{Threshold}} \right)$$

Take action
Forward message

3.7 RESULT AND DISCUSSION

Figure 3.8 shows the graph of message forwarding rate with the respective time (second) of the proposed system (secure and relevance VANET), which is greater than that of the existing system (VANET). Rate of message forwarding is calculated using the following formula:

$$\text{IMF} = \frac{\sum \text{Received Message}}{\sum \text{Sent Message}} \times 100 \tag{3.4}$$

3.8 ANALYSIS OF PRIORITY-BASED MESSAGE DELIVERY

Figure 3.9 shows the graph of priority message delivery with the respective time (ms). Here five different priority messages are considered from the existing and proposed systems. From graph, it is seen that higher-priority messages are received first and it takes lesser time than the existing scheme.

Time interval between sending messages by source nodes and receiving message at the destination end is calculated using the following formula:

$$\text{Priority Based Message} \left(P, T \right) = \int_{i=0}^{T} \left[\text{Recvd } Pkt_{\text{Time}} - \text{Sent } Pkt_{\text{Time}} \right]_{P} dT \tag{3.5}$$

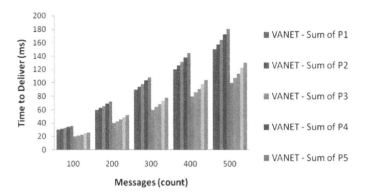

FIGURE 3.9   Priority-based message forwarding rate with respect to time.

Where
P=priority message
T=time of simulator

Figure 3.9 shows the graph of five different priority messages and their required time to reach at destination. Relevance-based VANET message forwarding scheme requires less time as compared to the existing scheme in VANET.

Figure 3.10 shows the time required for delivery of each type of priority messages.

3.9 CONCLUSION

From the result analysis and explained theory of the proposed scheme, we can conclude that intelligent message forwarding scheme has the following benefits:

• Highest-priority messages reach first to the destination.
• Scheme preserves the message integrity by hash function.
• Scheme retains nonreputation by checking the validity of source node.
• Fake events are blocked from forwarding.
• Authentic node can only forward messages.

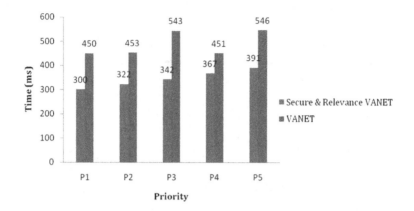

FIGURE 3.10   Priority message delivery time.

REFERENCES

1. X. Li and H. Li, "A survey on data dissemination in VANETs", *Chinese Science Bulletin*, vol. 59, no. 32, p. 4190, 2014.
2. H. Zhang and Z.-P. Jiang, "Modeling and performance analysis of ad hoc broadcasting schemes", *Performance Evaluation*, vol. 63, pp. 1196–1215, 2006. Elsevier.
3. J. P. Ryu, M.-S. Kim, S.-H. Hwang, and K.-J. Han, "An Adaptive Probabilistic Broadcast Scheme for Ad-Hoc Networks", *High Speed Networks and Multimedia Communications* (Eds., Z. Mammeri, P. Lorenz), pp. 646–654. Springer, Cham, 2004.
4. D. Lee, S. Chang, and S. Lee, "Analysis and design on efficient message relay methods in VANET", *Multimedia Tools and Applications*, vol. 74, no. 16, p. 6331, 2015. Springer.
5. H. Zhang and Z.-P. Jiang, "Performance analysis of broadcasting schemes in mobile ad hoc networks", *IEEE Communications Letters*, vol. 8, no. 12, pp. 718–720, 2004.
6. A. T. Giang, A. Busson and V. Vèque, "Message dissemination in VANET: Protocols and performances", In *Wireless Vehicular Networks for Car Collision Avoidance*, pp. 71–96, 2013.
7. W. Brad and C. Tracy, "Comparison of broadcasting techniques for mobile ad hoc networks", In *Proceedings of the 3rd ACM Symposium on Mobile Adhoc Networking & Computing,* Lausanne, Switzerland, 2002.
8. B. Williams, D. P. Mehta, et al., "Predictive models to rebroadcast in mobile ad hoc networks", *IEEE Transactions On Mobile Computing*, vol. 3, no. 3, pp. 295–303, 2004.

9. J. Yoo et al., "INK: Implicit neighbor knowledge routing in ad hoc networks", In *57th IEEE Semiannual Vehicular Technology Conference,* Jeju, Korea (South), South Korea, 2003.
10. C. Adler, S. Eichler, T. Kosch, et al., "Self-organized and context-adaptive information diffusion in vehicular adhoc networks", In *3rd International Symposium on Wireless Communication Systems,* Valencia, Spain, 2006.
11. S. P. Godse and P. N. Mahalle, "Intelligent authentication and message forwarding in VANET". *International Journal of Smart Vehicles and Smart Transportation (IJSVST),* vol. 3, no. 1, pp. 1–20, 2020. doi:10.4018/IJSVST.2020010101
12. F. Cunha, L. Villas, et al., "Data communication in VANETs: Application and challenges", *Ad Hoc Networks,* vol. 44, pp. 90–103, 2016. Elsevier.
13. C. Suthaputchakun, et al. "Priority based inter-vehicle communication in vehicular ad-hoc networks using IEEE 802.11e", In *IEEE 2007,* Dublin, Ireland, pp. 2595–2599, 2007.
14. H. Wu, R. Fujimoto, et al., "MDDV: A mobility-centric data dissemination algorithm for vehicular networks", In *VANET'04,* Philadelphia, Pennsylvania, USA, pp. 47–56, October 1, 2004.
15. C. Ghorai, et al., "A Novel Priority Based Exigent Data Diffusion Approach for Urban VANets", In *ICDCN 17,* Hyderabad, India, January 4–7, 2017.
16. A. Betsy Felicia, et al. "Accident avoidance and privacy preserving navigation system in vehicular network", *International Journal of Engineering Science and Computing,* vol. 6, pp. 2266–2270, March 2016.
17. T. W. Chim, et al. "VSPN: VANET-based secure and privacy-preserving navigation", *IEEE Transactions on Computers,* vol. 63, no. 2, pp. 510–524, 2014.
18. S. E. Carpenter, "Balancing safety and routing efficiency with VANET beaconing messages", In *National Highway Traffic Safety Administration, Fatality Analysis Reporting System (FARS) Encyclopedia,* October 15, 2013.
19. R. Frank, et al. "Bluetooth low energy: An alternative technology for VANET applications", In *2014 11th Annual Conference on Wireless on-Demand Network Systems and Services (WONS),* Obergurgl, Austria, IEEE, 2014.
20. M. Monir, A. Abdel-Hamid, and M. Abd El Aziz. "A categorized trust-based message reporting scheme for VANETs", In *Advances in Security of Information and Communication Networks* (Eds., A. I. Awad, A. E. Hassanien, K. Baba), pp. 65–83. Springer, Heidelberg, 2013.
21. A. Rao, et al. "Secure V2V communication with certificate revocations". *2007 Mobile Networking for Vehicular Environments,* Klaipeda City, Lithuania, IEEE, 2007.

Challenges in VANET

4

4.1 VOLATILITY

Due to high speed of vehicles, VANET (vehicular ad hoc network) is a highly volatile network. Connection between vehicles remains for a very short time period. Connection and disconnection between nodes is a continuous activity [6]. Also, nodes are moving in opposite directions, which makes the network more volatile. Due to volatility, VANET faces the following challenges.

4.1.1 Maintain Communication on Move

Due to volatility of a network, nodes in the network move randomly and loose connections that are established for communication. Disconnections of nodes cause an interruptions in the previous data packet transmission. It is important to establish a new path between the source and the destination if nodes loss their connection. It adds extra overhead in dynamic networks like VANET. So, it is a challenging task to maintain the communication between the nodes on move.

4.1.2 Delivery of Message Should Be in Short Time

VANET nodes remain in the vicinity of each other for a short time period. Therefore, the time interval between sending message from the source and receiving it by the receiver should be short. It is always a challenging job to achieve low latency in vehicular communication.

4.1.3 High-Speed Routing

Routing is the process of finding path between the source and the destination for communication. As nodes are moving, it is a challenging task to adapt the existing wireless routing protocols as per VANET environment. Connection and disconnection between nodes initiate rerouting frequently. Fast routing plays a crucial role to achieve successful communication and to avoid wastage of the effort already taken for communication.

4.1.4 Real-Time Selection of Alternative Communication Path

Rerouting process is initiated frequently in VANET due to volatility. Finding alternative communication path among the available path is challenging as it not only depends on the distance between nodes but also needs to consider the velocity, direction, and density of nodes. So a real-time selection of path in VANET is a topic of research.

4.2 CRITICAL TIME LATENCY OF MESSAGES DELIVERY

Latency is nothing but the time interval between sending message by the source node and receiving messages by the receiver node. In VANET, highly mobile nodes, i.e., vehicles, may be running in opposite directions. The nodes remain in the vicinity of each other for very short time periods. It is important to receive the message by the destination vehicle in a given time period. To achieve this communication, the network should satisfy the critical latency requirement. Communication in VANET network should be with low latency. It is a challenging task to achieve low latency while communication in VANET.

Safety message transmission is the main goal of the vehicular network. Safety messages should be always at higher priority, and it should be reached at destination on time. To achieve this feature needs to overcome a delay in network. The main challenges to overcome a delay in vehicular networks are as follows [1]:

- Frequency of changing neighborhood due to high mobility
- Drastically increasing load on network due to high-density environment

- Connectivity issue due to the variation in the received signal power
- Packet dropping due to exposed and hidden terminal problems.

4.3 DRASTIC INCREMENT IN VEHICLES AND ROADS

Road network in any country plays an important role in the development of country. Road networks in developing countries are drastically increasing every year. Every year millions of new vehicles are added to the network. The increasing number of vehicles and roads raises the following challenges in the VANET.

4.3.1 To Establish Required Infrastructure for New Roads

To provide VANET services on newly established roads, all essential devices like road side units (RSUs) and servers are needed to deploy. It is challenging to do for drastically increasing infrastructure. It needs both resources and cost of deployment.

4.3.2 Registration and Generation of Credentials for New Vehicles

Every new vehicle is registered with a trusted authority (TA). The TA provides certificates or necessary credentials to vehicles for using the network. Every vehicle has a unique identity, which is assigned by the TA. It is a challenging task to register and assign credential to the increasing number of vehicles. These credentials are also maintained by the TA throughout the lifespan of vehicles. Monitoring vehicles and providing some common services through the network are becoming tedious tasks if vehicles are increasing in million.

4.3.3 Slow Down the Performance of Network Due to the Increasing Number of Vehicles

The increasing number of vehicles puts extra overhead on the existing network. If an infrastructure is overloaded due to high density of vehicles, the performance of the network will decrease. The network may slow down. There is a need to update network resource capacity to achieve the required performance.

4.4 DIVERSE NETWORKING STANDARDS

VANET is an ad hoc network. VANET communication requirements differ from the other ad hoc networks. Protocols and standards available for the vehicular network are not applicable as it is to VANET. There is a need to adapt these standards as per a new requirement of VANET, or establish new standards. Both adapting existing standards and establishing new standards are challenging tasks. Selection of protocols from an available set of standard protocols is a challenging task. These selected protocols are used in different layers of communication model. The selection of protocol mainly depends on the vehicular environment of the particular region. These environments may differ in density of vehicles, road types (plain, hilly), number of lanes, rules of traffic, direction of vehicles, speed limit of vehicles, etc. It is a tough task to select the protocols for a given vehicular environment or adapt it for the required environment if it does not exist.

4.5 HIGH MOBILITY OF NODES

As we know, the nodes in vehicular network are the vehicles with high speed. It is a highly mobile network. Mobility of nodes is prone to the following challenges in the network.

4.5.1 Frequent Disconnection of Nodes in the Network

As nodes moves in different speeds, they connect and disconnect frequently. Disconnection of nodes causes an interruption in communication. Thus, it requires retransmission of data. Disconnection may cause data loss and time delay in sending data at the receiver end. It degrades the performance of the network. It is a challenging task to provide network rerouting and overcome a disconnection effect.

4.5.2 Frequently Changing Topology

The mobility of nodes causes frequently changing topology.

4.5.3 Data Retransmission If Communication Fails

Failure in communication needs to retransmit data to the receiver node. Extra overheads are required for retransmission of data. It occupies both resources and bandwidth of the network. It also causes a delay in receiving messages.

4.5.4 Low Packet Delivery Ratio

Packet delivery ratio (PDR) is used as a parameter to measure the performance of network. It is a ratio of number of packets received at the receiver end divided by the number of packets sent by the source node. Due to high mobility of nodes, the PDR is affected as communication is interrupted frequently.

4.6 NETWORK SECURITY

In VANET, a vehicle is nothing but intelligent mobile node, which communicates with its neighbors in the network; neighbors can be vehicles or RSUs. Here, we presented different approaches to further improve the security, robustness, and efficiency of the overall VANET system (Figure 4.1).

4.6.1 VANET Security Requirements

1. **Certification:** Certification/authentication authenticates the source node and ensures that only valid nodes can send messages and attackers' intent can be reduced in larger manner. Authentication method should
   - Authenticate node
   - Not disclose nodes' privacy
   - Be very efficient and less time-consuming.

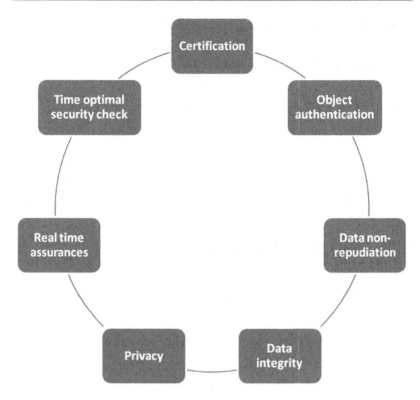

FIGURE 4.1   VANET security requirements.

2. **Data integrity:** Message integrity is nothing but ensuing messages are not changed in between the network transits. In message integrity, it should be ensured that when any driver receives message, that should not be false or wrong [7,8].

3. **Data non-repudiation:** Message/data non-repudiation ensures the sender can't deny about the same node that sends the message. While doing this, any message non-repudiation should be checked by only permitted authenticated authorities, not by any one [7,8].

4. **Object/entity authentication:** Entity authentication ensures that actual message sender and message sender defined in the message should be the same. And that the sender can be identified in a certain given area in a short time span [8].

5. **Data/message confidentiality:** Message confidentiality ensures that message can be received and sent by authenticated and private nodes. Third party can't see that message.

6. **Privacy:** Privacy ensures that message is only accessed and viewed by the authenticated users, and third party or unauthorized user can't view this message. Also, any other nodes can track vehicles' location and their queries asked to authorities [7].

7. **Real-time assurances:** Time guarantee is very important aspect in any VANET real-time applications. This can be achieved by protocols, methods, or applications to ensure time sensitivity.

8. **Time-optimal security check:** VANET is a dense network where nodes are more in short area. And those all nodes should be authenticated in a very short time span. Ensuring fast authentication is very important to serve more vehicles by authorities.

4.6.2 Problems in VANET Security

VANET security and VANET problems can be defined as different security breaches, which violate the aforementioned security requirements. These security violations occurred because of various reasons, and those can be defined in three parts [2,3]:

1. What are the security challenges?
2. What are the security adversaries that attack VANET?
3. What are the properties that support security issues?

4.6.2.1 Security Challenges

- **Authentication and privacy:** Every message should be verified, and its node gets authenticated before it gets delivered to the respective destination. Also while doing this, privacy of both nodes and messages should be maintained.
- **High vehicle density and high mobility:** RSU and authority servers have heavy load because of a large number of vehicles, messages, and their authentication. So, here authentication time should be minimized to serve more vehicles and messages in a given time.
- **Real-time message delivery:** VANET applications are mainly used to notify events like accidents, traffic, and weather condition, so the applications should follow the strict message delivery time and those messages should be delivered on a given priority basis.
- **Location awareness:** Attacks like Sybil can be identified by knowing its original node location, and also, many applications required vehicle location, which should be tracked to provide better services. This can be managed by secure GPS services.

4.6.2.2 Attacks

- **Greedy drivers or businesses:** Most of the drivers are honest and follow traffic routes but exception where drivers want to use more of the available resources to get edge in business or self-priorities. Like, drivers generate false message about accidents or hazards conditions, so other vehicles divert their vehicles and then those routes can be used fully by those greedy drivers.

  Message delay is one type of attack whenever required messages should be delivered on time to avoid issues in network like accidents or traffic congestion.

- **Snoops/eavesdroppers:** These people try to get unauthorized extra information about others. They can get identify of other vehicle or hack the system to get a required information.

- **Pranksters:** Pranksters are mostly teenagers; to get fun, they send wrong message to other vehicles which misguide them and turn to adverse situations. Also some time, they use Distributed Denial of Service (DDoS) attack to delay to stop messages.

- **Industrial insiders:** Hardware manufacturers install a firmware that breaks security and steals data. This kind of security breaches are very difficult to find and dangerous for VANET. Also using tampering devices attacker can stole other vehicle's identity and keys. Intruder in their network can breach the security and access unauthorized data.

- **Malicious attackers:** Attackers cause harm to the vehicular network, which is the most important concern for our security system. These attackers are more professionals, and they know loop holes in the system. They can attack by using techniques like Sybil attack, replay attack, DDoS attack, and false messages.

4.6.2.3 Properties

VANET has very special properties in this network, which are very special for security.

- **In-built high processing power and ample power supply:** Vehicles come with their own batteries, and OBUs (on-board units) have high processing power. So, taking security measures and implementing security checks/algorithms are somewhat suitable compared to

MANET (mobile ad hoc network), where the most challenging issue is power shortage.

* **Can track location and known time:** There is a continuous communication between RSU and TA, it's easy to track its current location using GPS and time. By using this location and time information, several algorithms can be implemented to track malicious nodes, Sybil attack, etc.
* **Periodic maintenance and inspection:** In periodic check, authorized agencies can regularly check for firmware software and avoid privacy issues. Also, authorities frequently change its key and other secure information from OBU.
* **Centralized certificate authority:** In MANET, there is no any provision for centralized registration process compared to VANET. Each vehicle should be registered with centralized agencies and has its own unique identity given by TA.
* **Existing law and infrastructure:** Existing law let attacker avoid security breaches, and if any attacks are found in the system, the current law can catch them and punish them for their wrong doing.

4.6.3 VANET Security Essential Parts

* **Vehicle black box:** Tamper proof device which is responsible for storing vehicles and all critical electronic data like speed, time, messages, and location.
* **Trusted component (TC):** Cryptographic keys are the most important to secure cryptographic operation, and to store keys needs a proper hardware protection. Trusted component is nothing but secure hardware that helps to store cryptographic keys in secure vault.
* **Unique ID for vehicles:** Vehicles' unique IDs are provided as electronic license plates, which helps to automate vehicle checkup and verification.
* **Key management system:** In key management system (KMS), TA plays an important role of issuing credential like public and private keys pairs to all registered vehicles. In case of larger region, there will be several TAs corresponding to different regions; TAs are verifying to each other for authenticity. Vehicle manufactures can also play the role of TAs.

4.7 EFFICIENT MESSAGE FORWARDING

1. VANET is the real-time network. On-time message delivery in the vehicular network is very important. Message forwarding in VANET is very crucial as it directly affects the runtime traffic control like avoiding congestions of vehicles, avoiding accidents, and informing driver about emergency situations, bad weather conditions. Efficient message forwarding scheme categorizes the message as per their importance and forwards the highest-priority messages first. It improves the message forwarding rate. Highest-priority message reached at destination in a required time. This can forward the highest-priority messages first. It is a challenging task to decide priorities of messages. Currently, our scheme applies our knowledge, experiences, runtime updates by environmental center, and different predictions. But there is a need to study and analyze various region traffic data with different parameters to decide priority of messages.

2. It is helpful to drivers for taking emergency decisions. As vehicles in the network are flooded with different types of messages at a time, it is necessary to dispatch higher-priority messages first.

3. Efficient message forwarding needs to tackle with the following changes in traditional message forwarding strategies.

   a. Categorization of messages as per their types
   b. Assigning priority to messages
   c. Establishing mechanism for dissemination of messages as per priority
   d. Analyzing results of message forwarding with priority.

These steps are used to implement priority-based message forwarding scheme. In Chapter 3, we have already studied the types of messages and different schemes for forwarding messages. It also explained new priority-based message forwarding scheme and in detail analysis of this scheme.

4.8 MITIGATION TECHNIQUES TO ADDRESS VANET SECURITY

VANET is vulnerable due to its open nature. Different types of attacks can be possible on the vehicular network. Depending on properties of attacker nodes, attacks can be classified into different types, as shown in Figure 4.2. We already saw some of the attacks in Section 4.6.2.2.

1. **Location-based attack:** Depending on locations of attacker node, attacks are classified into two types: insider and outsider attack.
   a. **Insider:** It is an authenticated node, which has valid credential and authority to communicate with other nodes in the vehicular network. This node may launch attack with his personal intention or without purpose attacks in network.
   b. **Outsider:** It is an unauthenticated node, not having permission to communicate with nodes in network. This node may stole credential of the authorized node and launches attacks intentionally or unintentionally to break down the network.
2. **Intention-based attack:** Some attackers carry out attacks with personal intentions. Others may carry out attacks without personal intentions.
   a. **Malicious:** Without any personal intention or benefit, this attacker node tries various methods to break down the network. As the attacker uses different methods or their combinations, the pattern of attack is unpredictable.
   b. **Rational:** The attacker node launches attacks for his personal benefit, i.e., intention. It follows some common pattern; these attacks are predictable.
3. **Harmfulness-based attack:**
   a. **Active:** These attackers change the packets on transmission. As information is getting changes in between, these attacks are more harmful to the network.
   b. **Passive:** These attackers does not make any changes in packets. They eavesdrop the packets or violate the privacy by reading information in between.
4. **Scope-based attack:** Depending on scope of attackers to launch the attack, it is classified as local and extended.

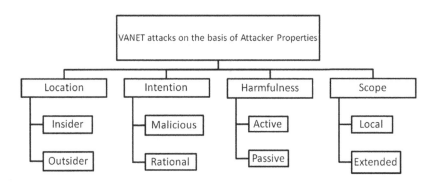

FIGURE 4.2   Classification of attacks in VANET.

a. **Local:** If the attacker's scope is limited to one based station or vehicle or any region, it is called a local attack.

b. **Extended:** If the attacker node has a broad scope and can control different entities in the network, it is called an extended attack.

There are different types of attacks under each type of attack categories. Here, general methods to mitigate/prevent each type of attack are introduced in brief.

- **Sybil attack:** In this attack, attacker node shows the multiple appearances in network. It may steal identities of multiple nodes or single node, and shows it at different locations. It sends fake messages from different locations. It looks like there are multiple nodes on road. It can be either insider or outsider node that can launch a Sybil attack.

- **Mitigation techniques used for Sybil attack:** Traditionally, three techniques are used: registration, position verification, and radio resource testing. Registration is not sufficient as attacker node registers with multiple identities by stealing other node identities and shows at its own.

In position verification, locations of nodes are verified from time to time, as it can't be moved beyond the limit. If nodes show multiple locations in a short time span, it will be detected as malicious node.

In radio resource testing, puzzles are given to nodes for solving if node entities solve puzzles in time and so it is considered as genuine. In case of Sybil attack, the attacker node shows multiple identities or single identities at multiple locations, so it receives multiple puzzles and fails to solve them. It detects as malicious nodes.

Public key infrastructure for VANETs (VPKI) is suggested, which detects and prevents Sybil attack using public key cryptography.

- **Time stamp approach:** This approach works if vehicle has RSU infrastructure. Idea of this approach is that two vehicles rarely pass through different RSUs located at far distances from each other at the same time. In this scheme, RSU assign time stamps to a vehicle that passes through its range. Messages forwarded by the vehicle contain several time stamps of previously passed RSUs. If multiple messages consist of very similar series of time stamp, it is detected as Sybil messages that are originated from a single vehicle. These are some techniques used to mitigate/prevent Sybil attack in the vehicular network.

- **Bogus information attack:** Attacker node sends bogus or fake information in the network for self-benefit. This attack can be insider or outsider attack. For example, attacker node passes message that there is heavy traffic ahead, even there is no such scenario for self-benefit.
- **Mitigation techniques used for bogus information attack:** This attack is detected or prevented by elliptic curve digital signature algorithm (ECDSA). ECDSA is message authentication scheme variant of digital signature algorithm (DSA). It uses hashing techniques for message security. In this technique, two keys are used: public key and private key. Public key is making available to each vehicle, and private key is a secret key with vehicle. Source and destination vehicles are agreed upon elliptic curve domain parameter for private key generation. Transmissions of message source node encrypt the message by using hash function and private key, and send to the destination node. At the destination node, message is decrypted using public key. It is stronger technique to avoid bogus information.
- **Denial-of-service attack (DOS):** It is the most common attack in the network. In this attack, malicious nodes send unwanted messages in the network and make network busy. Because of this, authentic nodes are prevented from accessing resources. The aim of the attack is to provide denial of resources services to legitimate node.
- **Mitigation techniques used for DOS attack:** The authors developed a model for DoS prevention called IP-CHOCK that provides the significant strength in locating malicious nodes without the requirement of any secret information exchange or special hardware support. Simulation results depict an encouraging detection rate that will be even enhanced whenever optimal numbers of nodes are forged by the attackers.
- **Black hole attack:** In this attack, attacker node generates the highest sequence number and shows the shortest path to destination. As source node receives an immediate first response from the attacker node, it starts sending message packets to attacker nodes. Attacker nodes drop packets after receiving them from source node without forwarding to the next hop.
- **Mitigation techniques used for black hole attack:** Intrusion detection system based on a real-time behavior or logs maintained by different resources in the network can handle the detection and prevention of these kinds of attack.
- **Gray hole attack:** It is a variation of black hole attack where the attacker node misleads the network by some time forwarding the

message packets like normal node, and some time forwarding the drop packets.

- **Mitigation techniques used for gray hole attack:** This attack uses the same intrusion detection system with changes as per gray hole symptoms.

These are some attacks that come under different categories of attack that we have seen. Here, we have discussed in short about attacks on VANET and their mitigation techniques.

REFERENCES

1. Z. Y. Rawashdeh and S. M. Mahmud, "Communications in Vehicular Networks" in Title Mobile Ad-Hoc Networks: Applications, Detroit, Michigan, USA: Wayne State University.
2. G. Samara, W. A. H. Al-Salihy, et al., "Security issues and challenges of vehicular adhoc networks (VANET)", In *4th International Conference on New Trends in Information Science and Service Science*, Gyeongju, pp. 393–398, 2010.
3. M. K. Nasir, A.S. M. Delowar Hossain, et al., "Security challenges and implementation mechanism for vehicular ad hoc network", *International Journal of Scientific & Technology Research*, vol. 2, no. 4, pp. 156–161, 2013.
4. S. P. Godse and P. N. Mahalle, "Rising issues in VANET communication and security: A state of art survey", *International Journal of Advanced Computer Science and Applications (IJACSA)*, vol. 8, no. 9, pp. 245–252, 2017.
5. S. P. Godse and P. N. Mahalle, "A computational analysis of ECC based novel authentication scheme in VANET", *International Journal of Electrical and Computer Engineering (IJECE)* vol. 8, no. 6, pp. 5268–5277, December 2018.
6. S. P. Godse and P. N. Mahalle, (2020). "Intelligent authentication and message forwarding in VANET", *International Journal of Smart Vehicles and Smart Transportation (IJSVST)*, vol. 3, no. 1, pp. 1–20. doi:10.4018/IJSVST.2020010101.
7. M. S. Sheik and J. Liang, "A comprehensive survey on VANET security services in traffic management system", *Wireless Communications and Mobile Computing*, vol. 2019, Article ID 2423915, 23 p.
8. M. Raya, P. Papadimitratos, and J.-P. Hubaux, "Securing vehicular communications", In *IEEE Wireless Communications Magazine, Special Issue on Inter-Vehicular Communications*, October 2006.

Scope and Application of VANET

5

5.1 SCOPE OF VANET

Vehicular network is a real-time ad hoc network. It provides an easy way of communication between vehicles on road and road side units (RSUs). It has a wide scope in intelligent transportation system (ITS). Before stating the applications of VANET, it's very important to see where and why the vehicular network will be useful.

5.1.1 Road Traffic Management Services

In the current scenario of road traffic management, traffic signals play an important role in controlling the traffic on road. Traffic signal system is based on the time event. It uses red, green, and yellow signals for traffic control. It uses time event, i.e., fixed time slots for changing signals. It may cause unnecessary waiting of vehicles on road due to red signal. Detecting a faulty vehicle and assigning a fine mechanism is depending on human resources and quality of camera. Checking the authentication and expiry date of a vehicle is manually done by human resources. Availability of human resources and cost of their monthly salary are also big issues. To overcome these issues, VANET will be a good solution. It can be helpful to automate these services by detecting different events on road and passing messages to the respective vehicle or control center based on the events. The following are some road services which can be possible under traffic management using VANET.

VANET is used to control traffic using traffic signal, navigate emergency vehicles, detect faulty vehicles, authenticate vehicles, detect the expiration of vehicles, and assign fine as per the consequence of disobeying traffic rules.

5.1.2 Commercial Application Services

These services involve a payment system or manual collection of money for providing services. In the current scenario, toll plaza services are available and involve human resources to collect money. In future, different services can be under the VANET commercial service scope: to collect toll at toll plaza, provide a location information on request, provide the shortest path based on distance and runtime traffic analysis, provide the location of consumer services as per ratings, and provide multimedia data like movie/song on request.

5.1.3 Road Safety Services

Road accidents and traffic jams are serious issues in any country's road transportation system. Consider you are traveling and your vehicle has a facility for receiving and sending messages. The vehicle will get emergency messages like traffic jam, an accident that has happened on road, bad weather, bad road, and location path in advance through a wireless medium. The vehicle can also request for information like path, map, and multimedia data. It is an amazing experience that makes driving comfortable, avoids accidents, and reduces wastage of time. In future, different services can be under the VANET safety service scope: it gives a safety-related message while the vehicle is moving on road, and it also gives messages like accident that has happened, sudden break applied by the next vehicle, traffic jam ahead, bad weather, and bad road condition.

VANET has a wide scope in all aforementioned services. As technologies and networks grow day-by-day, some more services will be added to it.

5.2 APPLICATION OF VANET

ITS provides a very robust and flexible way of communication between vehicles and road-side infrastructure, which helps to come up with various applications and services for VANET users. This new communication technology of vehicle-to-infrastructure communication brings an opportunity to develop applications for public services on road. VANET applications are mainly divided into the following types:

1. Road safety applications
2. Traffic management
3. User-oriented services
4. Convenience services.

5.2.1 Road Safety Applications

Road safety applications involve monitoring traffic and road, communicating with other vehicles, gathering or sharing information about road surface and curves etc. Road safety applications can be categorized as:

1. Real-time traffic monitoring
2. Cooperative message exchange
3. Broadcast messaging for event notifications
4. Road safety/status notifications
5. Track driver offenses.

5.2.1.1 Real-Time Traffic Monitoring

5.2.1.1.1 Advanced Safety Vehicle
In Japan, between 1996 and 2000, the advanced safety vehicle (ASV) was developed to provide the detection and prevention of collision and navigation system [1]. The demo was established to provide a cooperative driver support system that uses 5.8-GHz band frequency and carrier-sense multiple access (CSMA) protocols for communication. In the same year, the advanced driver assistance systems (ADAS) project was developed to support Advance Cruise Control and Collision Avoidance Systems. The ASV project was, then, extended to ASV-3 and ASV-4 in 2001 and 2005, respectively [2].

5.2.1.1.2 Road Traffic Signaling System
In 2012, research was proposed for road traffic signaling. The road traffic signaling system is based on a VANET's distributed schema. The system transfers the real-time information from different roads and vehicles to get a better traffic flow, reduce congestion, and optimize journey time. It uses wireless sensor network (WSN) and radio-frequency identification (RFID), as well as video and image processing. It relies on WAVE for the communications between vehicles. The vehicles are equipped with on-board units (OBUs) [3].

5.2.1.1.3 Intelligent Road Traffic Monitoring and Management System
Intelligent road traffic monitoring and management system (IRTMMS) was introduced in 2015 based on VANET's communication in Ref. [4]. The IRTMMS adopts an intelligent traffic signal that uses an unscheduled signaling scheme to optimize the signal durations by estimating the real-time traffic. The final destination of a vehicle is informed by the vehicle. OBUs use destination along with roads to that destination and calculate the load on different roads to reduce congestions [4].

5.2.1.1.4 SDN-Based Real-Time Urban Traffic Analysis
The research proposed a data-driven approach that implements an artificially intelligent model for predicting the vehicular traffic behavior. The used architecture is based on two models: the first is the software-defined networking (SDN) with improved scalability, flexibility, and adaptability. The SDN is amended by the software-defined vehicular network (SDVN) architecture. The second approach is based on a machine-learning algorithm that aims to efficiently model the traffic flow. The research focuses on solving traffic congestion by using neural network learning abilities and VANET-based algorithms to predict the future traffic densities [5].

5.2.2 Cooperative Message Exchange

Vehicles can take a cooperative poll for any behavior and share those messages to each other. This type of message many times is used for the detection of malicious vehicles. Once the vehicle or node is detected as a malicious one, a list of such type of malicious vehicles is shared with other vehicles in the network. These messages are used to detect and prevent attacks on the network. Attacker nodes can disturb the network by passing fake messages, which can misguide vehicles to take an unwanted decision. This decision can result in wastage of time or loss of life of passenger traveling in that vehicle. It also hacks data and important messages that are sent to the authentic vehicles in the network. It creates an issue of privacy and future data misuses. Considering these security issues, cooperative messages play an important role in the vehicular network.

5.2.3 Broadcast Messaging for Events Notification

Broadcasting is used when messages are applicable to all nodes in the network. Such types of messages are common to all nodes in the vehicular network. In the vehicular network, various information is provided by the trusted authority (TA) to RSUs and vehicles. This information is applicable to all nodes under TA. RSU also holds information which is used for authentication of vehicles. RSU also holds CRL (Certification Revocation List) list to check the validity of vehicles. It is broadcasted in the network if required [6].

In the vehicular network, different events may be detected by vehicles on move. Once a vehicle detects an event and confirms a reality of the event (like accident that has happened on road, bad weather, and bad road conditions), those event messages are generated by the vehicle and broadcasted into the network.

5.2.4 Road Safety/Status Notifications

Road safety messages are important in considering the safety point of view of vehicles on move. Different routes can be available to the same destination. Some routes are the shortest but are prone to bad condition. These roads are dangerous for traveling. These notifications can be provided to the vehicle on move by RSU or the next vehicle which is already on the same road. It also provides safety instructions to the driver while move, like sudden turn, long curve, slope ahead, diversion, speed beaker, and tunnel ahead. It is helpful to alert driver priorly and avoid accident-like situations. Road status messages are generated by RSUs or vehicles if traffic jam situation occurs, accident has happened ahead, or road is closed due to some reasons. It will help to prevent further traffic jam and inconvenience of passengers.

5.2.5 Track Driver Offenses

A vehicle's driver is responsible for all behaviors of the vehicle on road. Some behaviors of the vehicle on road are treated as offenses, like crossing speed limit, overtaking from wrong side, not following lane rules, driving in wrong direction, driving without license, and steeling private information of other drivers. These are some serious issues while traveling on road. Misbehavior of a driver can be tracked by the collected data, and instructions or warnings will be provided by the road authority to such offenses.

5.3 TRAFFIC MANAGEMENT

Traffic management comes with tasks like checking traffic density, notifying other vehicles with broadcasting event messages, pre-notifying to avoid collision, and reroute options

1. Priority-based messaging
2. Reroute option notifications

3. Collision avoidance messages
4. Lane guidance
5. Emergency notifications.

5.3.1 Priority-Based Messaging

Nodes in a vehicular network are flooded with different types of messages at runtime. It is very important to decide the highest-priority messages among these types. Classifying the messages and assigning priorities to messages are challenging tasks. In priority-based messaging, each message is assigned with a priority value, which depends on the severity of message. Nodes that receive message are deployed with priority-checking mechanism. Among all the messages, vehicle/RSU forwarding is the first highest-priority message.

5.3.2 Rerouting Option Notifications

Road transport is full of uncertainty; many situations (accident that has happened on road, heavy traffic jam, natural calamities that occur due to rainy, fog, or wind, etc) occur on road which interrupt a regular flow of vehicles on road. If vehicles that traveling on the same road and located on few kilometer from actual event locations, it is better to choose some other route to avoid the loss of time. Vehicle that caught in such situation can request a new route information to other vehicles or RSUs. Sometime RSU/TA broadcasts accident and reroutes information to all vehicles which are on the same road. Reroute option is also useful to emergency vehicles that provide emergency services at event locations.

5.3.3 Collision Avoidance Messages

Collision of vehicles on road is the main reason of accident. Vehicles collide with each other because of the sudden break applied by the preceding vehicle, wrong side overtaking, losing the control of vehicle due to high speed, vehicle not visible due to a sudden turn, and driving at night time where vehicles are not clearly visible to each other. This collision can be avoided if vehicle gets information about the speed of the next vehicle, distancing between vehicles surrounded to it, break applied by the next vehicle, peak turn etc. Collision avoidance messages contain these kinds of information and communicate among vehicles around it. This information prevents the accident by avoiding collision of vehicles.

5.3.4 Lane Guidance

Express way and highways are provided with multiple lanes for different types of vehicles. Each lane has a speed limit and rules for overtaking. If a vehicle disobeys the rules of lane, it may cause accidents. Lane rules are monitored and notified to the vehicles on road. Lane guidance is helpful for new vehicles which do not have sufficient information about rules and regulations of a particular lane.

5.3.5 Emergency Notifications

As we have already seen, road transportation is prone to many emergency situations like accident that has happened ahead, traffic jam ahead, bad road conditions, bad weather, and natural calamities due to bad weather. These emergency notifications are provided by the vehicle or road authority. Emergency notification will avoid further traffic jam and accidental situation. It saves the time and life of passenger.

5.4 USER-ORIENTED SERVICES

User-oriented services come under nonsafety messages. These services are preferred by the user to make his traveling comfortable and easy. Services like request for movie, audio songs, location information, navigation, data, and web access come under this category.

5.4.1 Personalized Vehicle Settings

Nowadays, research in vehicle automation is on peak. Driverless car is also available with a specific infrastructure. Personalized vehicle settings will control different tasks of user which were previously controlled by vehicle users manually. It covers cruise control, speed control, lane tracing, and different alerts to users about internal and external appliances of vehicle. These vehicle settings are used for semi-automation or fully automation of vehicle functionalities.

5.4.2 Web Access

Internet is the main source of connectivity with world. It provides different information and updates to user. Web accessibility services can be requested by user while traveling. These services are provided by VANET upon a user request. Web services are provided by devices deployed along road sides.

5.4.3 Usage of Map

Traveling in different geographical areas becomes easy and comfortable if you are with an exact map of those locations. Navigation system also uses a map to track the roads to reach at destination. Navigation and maps are more advanced these days, which provide the shortest path between the source and the destination. The shortest path-finding algorithms consider runtime traffic, distance, and condition of road to select the shortest path.

5.4.4 Real-Time Audio/Video Streaming

Real-time audio or video data may be requested by the passenger. Audio/video data streaming requires a high-speed network. It can involve videos that fetch for entertainment, informative video, advertisement, important announcement, voice along with video conversation with vehicles in the network, navigation videos/audio from the remote location etc.

5.4.5 Advertisement

The vehicular network is a broader network that contains millions of vehicles worldwide. And it carries billions of passengers daily. This well-established vehicular network is a good source of advertisements. It is utilized for government and private ads. Advertisements are posted on dashboard to get information about a government scheme or product. It can be useful for publicity and awareness of quality products.

5.5 CONVENIENCE SERVICES

Convenience services improve the traffic efficiency by providing useful services to drivers: it is basically helpful to automate and speed up the services on the road network. At the end, these services help to reduce time of waiting and achieve time and money saving.

5.5.1 Route Diversions

On a road network, diversions play a role in changing route. These diversions are confusing some time for drivers who are traveling for the first time on that road. If prior messages are provided to vehicles before diversion arrives, it will help to avoid misunderstanding of drivers and result in a right path selection. It is also helpful to avoid accidents, where a sudden diversion occurs.

5.5.2 E-toll Collections

E-tolls provide essential and unavoidable services to improve road network and road side infrastructure. Manually collecting money from each vehicle as per its category is a tedious task. It takes patience of driver waiting in toll plaza queue. It also increases the manual work of person who collects a money. VANET can be utilized to identify the vehicle type and deduct the money amount as per the charges of toll. It will save larger waiting time of vehicles. It also indirectly helps to save fuel, which in turn results in time and cost saving.

5.5.3 Notify about Parking

Parking is becoming the biggest problem in city and metropolitan city. Many times parking is not available in city. Smart parking is required for avoiding unnecessary queues at a parking slot. Sometimes a user comes to the parking place and parking is full. It is a worst-case scenario when a user is in queue and parking full, when his number comes. To avoid such scenarios, there is a need of prior reservation of parking slot by the vehicle owner. VANET can be used to broadcast information about parking locations and the availability of parking in different slots. Vehicle user can request for parking slot to parking admin; if slot is available, it can be booked by the vehicle user. This facility comes under commercial service of VANET.

5.5.4 Prediction Services

Prediction-based services depend on previous experiences and runtime data available. User can request about traffic-related prediction to select the road for journey. RSU can do the weather analysis and suggest some precautionary announcement to vehicles in the range of RSU. Some accident spots on roads are identified, and depending on the speed of vehicles at runtime, prediction safety messages can be given to vehicles.

5.6 POTENTIAL PROJECTS ON VANET

Here, we have given some sample projects that are completed or under research in the VANET domain.

5.6.1 "Wireless Traffic Service Platform for Linking Cars Project"

This project is an initiative taken by Eureka Celtic. It is developed to provide an intelligent wireless traffic service platform for cars on road. Under this platform, cars are made available with updates regarding weather conditions, urban traffic management, and different information of city. Cars on road can communicate with base station located besides the road. It uses a wireless network like Wi-Fi for communicating with base station. Cars can also communicate with each other under ad hoc scenario. Base station collects different weather information and forwards that information to the central unit. Central unit processes the data, provides weather information, traffic information etc., and updates to past cars through the base station.

This project uses approaches that extend the performances of WLANs, WiMAX. It also considers cellular network and transmission network technologies. Integrating all network technologies considers different scenarios in the vehicular network communication like vehicle to vehicle, vehicle to RSU, and RSU to RSU. It also takes care of network coverage and data transmission ability everywhere in the different regions/area of applications, like on highways, roads as well as urban street areas. Urgent information is provided by the system using low-rate wireless connection (via GPRS) between end users and central unit, to provide urgent information in real time. The coverage will be tested in various severe weather conditions with different topologies.

CARLINK equipment is developed for vehicles; it transmits the position of vehicles while they are on move, which helps to track the vehicles. It also collects the forecast weather and traffic conditions using various sensors. Collected information is used to take decisions in services on road. Services like weather information services and local traffic management services are provided by CARLINK. Other services can be added as per requirements.

5.6.2 "Providing Adaptive Ubiquitous Services in Vehicular Contexts"

SEISCIENTOS is a group project between the networking group of Valencia and the University of Murcia. This project is funded by the Spanish "Ministry of Science and Innovation" (MICINN).

This project is aimed to provide infrastructure and framework for providing communication services to end users in a ubiquitous vehicular environment. It makes available communications in vehicular networks like V2V and V2I. The networks explored on various communication technologies and tried to provide a common communication platform, isolating the user from handoffs or changes that may occur between different network technologies.

Work provides a common solution, for the activities providing services at the vehicle and infrastructure side. Traffic environment is adopted for both safety and comfort of passengers and drivers. These networks can take advantages of seamless access to a range of services in safety, entertainment, and information.

5.6.3 WiSafeCar "Wireless Traffic Safety Network Between Cars"

WiSafeCar is a Eureka Celtic Project jointly addressed by Luxembourg, Finland, France, Turkey, and Spain. The overall aim of this project is to provide reliable traffic services to the vehicle. It mainly focuses on traffic safety alert messages like accidents that has happened, traffic jam, and other data services to vehicles.

Project aims are achieved by secure data collection from vehicles and fixed stations. Collected data is utilized to make an analysis of traffic situations and other safety measures. Decisions and warnings based on the analysis made are provided to the real-time transport service applications. The objectives of this project are in accordance with those of Celtic's earlier project, CARLINK.

5.6.4 CVIS "Cooperative Vehicle-Infrastructure Systems"

The aim of this project is to design, develop, and test technologies required in a wireless communication environment for the vehicular network.

This system provides a cooperative infrastructure for wireless communication among vehicles and infrastructure. It is equipped with sensor detection technology to sense environmental and real-time road behavior of vehicles. Smart interaction between vehicle and infrastructure is achieved in this system. Due to an efficient resource utilization, safety road traveling, and reducing traffic jams, CVIS is a new trend for ITS. This system is designed to interpret the intention of participants at runtime. It not only guesses car's next activity, but also judges the situation accurately, so that car can take a right move.

In addition to interactive capabilities, CVIS improves the perception of autonomous vehicle drastically. Different sensors like vision, radar, and LiDAR are mounted on cars and street light poles, which evolve into all in one signal pole, all in one traffic pole, and all in one electric alarm pole. Due to perception future of car and road terminals, it helps to minimize blind zones by notifying a collision alert in advance to vehicle.

5.6.5 SAFESPOT: Smart Vehicles on Smart Roads

This is an integrated project cofunded by the European Commission Information Society Technologies.

1. **Aims of this system:**
   - To develop open communication platform by using infrastructure and the vehicles as sources and destinations of safety-related information.
   - To develop ad hoc dynamic network with accurate relative localization and dynamic local traffic maps.
   - To develop and test scenario-based applications in order to evaluate the impacts on road safety.
   - To define a sustainable deployment strategy for cooperative systems for road safety, and also evaluate related liability, regulations, and standardization aspects.
2. **Communicating elements used in the system:**
   - OBU deployed on vehicle
   - RSU along the fixed distances as per range of device
   - Traffic control unit that forwards safety and other information.
3. **Applications of system:**
   - Provides safety to road user.
   - Provides awareness to driver by safety measure at runtime.
   - Enables vehicle for handling critical situations on road.
   - Involves in the development of new safety applications based on the cooperative approach.

Vehicle and infrastructure-based applications are provided by SAFESPOT, which are as follows:

- Road intersection safety
- Lane change maneuver
- Safe overtaking
- Head-on collision warning
- Rear-end collision
- Speed limitation and safety distance
- Frontal collision warning
- Road condition status—slippery road
- Curve warning
- Vulnerable road user detection and accident avoidance.

The SAFESPOT infrastructure-based applications take decisions related to road infrastructure in cooperation with vehicles. The applications are as follows:

- Speed alert
- Hazard and incident warning
- Road departure prevention
- Intelligent cooperative intersection safety
- Safety margin for assistance and emergency vehicles.
- These applications aim to provide the most efficient recommendation to the driver through the on-board HMI and through road side communication devices like VMS or flashing lights.

5.7 TOOLS AND SIMULATION PLATFORM FOR VANET

5.7.1 System Modeling

Before developing or implementing any network, it should be tested with some simple way that is called system modeling. System model helps to represent how system performs when actually implemented. System model comes with test bed, takes different parameters, and executes a frequent analysis with different views.

System models help in the following ways:

1. Helps to test different parameters.
2. Analyzes and helps to build efficient system.

3. Makes learning system easy.
4. Reduces the cost of actual implementation.

Two modeling approaches are defined: analytical approach and simulation approach.

1. **Analytical approach:** Analytical approach first understands the system to be implemented and describes the system mathematically with the help of numerical methods, probabilities etc. This approach is simple, small, and with understandable proof is less preferable than simulation. Here, models are mathematically traceable and provide numerical solutions. To make this model successful requires lightweight computational efforts. This model is cost-effective and also helps to get an abstract view of the components, which show how different components interact with each other in the system.

2. **Simulation approach:** The mostly accepted and widely used model is simulation approach. It is applied in manufacturing, planning, engineering research, business analysis and biological science experimentation, network modeling, and many more. Compared to analytical modeling, this model is more presentable and accurate to execute, and helps to describe the actual system. If the proposed network model is large and complex, then it is very difficult to model using the analytical approach. In contrast, it is very easy to implement using the simulation approach. Analytical approach becomes unmanageable if the system is complex and large.

3. **Basics of computer network simulation:** To make simulation successful, we have to follow certain steps. Regardless of problems, objective, and process, these steps should be followed to make a simulation successful. Simulation comes with the following steps:
   * **Problem definition:** Defines goals and finds what needs to be solved.
   * **Project planning:** Defines different tasks, and creates workdown structure and schedule task; from this, we come to know how this simulation goes till end.
   * **System definition:** Defines components and analysis measure to analyze problem statements.
   * **Model formulation:** Defines how the actual system works and defines flowchart to show all function flows.
   * **Input data collection and analysis:** Get different result and do analysis.
   * **Model translation:** Using programming language implements this system

4. **Simulation:** The formal definition – According to Shannon [7], simulation is "the process of designing a model of a real system and conducting experiments with this model for the purpose of understanding the behavior of the system and/or evaluating various strategies for the operation of the system." With the dynamic nature of computer networks, we thus actually deal with a dynamic model of a real dynamic system.

5.7.2 Foundations of Simulation

- **Entities:** These are objects that participate in different network activities. Objects interact with one another in a simulation program. There interaction causes a change in system state. In the computer network, entities are nothing but computer nodes, packets, flows of packets, or nonphysical objects such as simulation clocks. Each object has unique attributes. Consider a packet entity, which has attributes such as packet length, sequence number, priority, and the header. Two objects are differentiated by their attribute values.

5.7.2.1 Resources

Any complex systems have resources to provide different services to objects in the system. Resources may be sharable or not sharable among entities. In general, a limited supply of resources has to be shared among a certain set of entities. In computer networks, sharable resources are bandwidth, air time, and the number of servers.

5.7.2.2 Activities and Events

Entities in the system are busy to do some activities. These activities may create different events. Events cause changes in the system. Change in the system is nothing but a change in state of system. This is a continuous process till the end state of any activity. Consider an ideal example of network activities like delay and queuing. If node needs to send a packet but finds the medium busy, it waits until the medium is free. In this case, the packet is to be sent over the air but the medium is busy, and the packet is said to be engaged in a waiting activity.

- **Scheduler:** It schedules the sequence of event execution. List of events and their execution time is predefined and maintained by scheduler. When simulation is in run state, scheduled events are executing as per their schedule time decided by scheduler.

5.7.2.3 Global Variable

It is very similar to global variable in programming. It is accessible by all functions or entities in the system. In simulation, it basically keeps track of some common values of the simulation. In computer networks, examples of global variable are length of the packet queue in a single-server network, the total busy air time of the wireless network, or the total number of packets transmitted.

- **Random number generator:** Random number generator (RNG) is used to generate randomness in a simulation model. It is generated by sequentially taking numbers from a deterministic sequence of pseudo-random number. Number selected from the sequence is appeared to be random. In some cases, pseudo-random sequence is predefined and used by every RNG. In some cases, RNG takes number from different locations of pseudo-random sequence. Location is called as seed. The actual implementation of RNG is initialized with seed. A seed identifies the starting location in a pseudo-random sequence from which RNG starts to pick numbers. In different simulations, seeds are different and thus generate different results. Consider an ideal example as computer network simulation, where packet arrival process, waiting process, and service process are usually modeled as random processes. A random process is expressed by sequences of random variables. These random processes are usually implemented with the aid of an RNG. for a comprehensive treatment on random process implementation (e.g., those having the uniform, exponential, Gaussian, Poisson, binomial distribution functions).
- **Statistics gatherer:** The responsibility of statistic gatherer is to collect a simulator-generated data. This data can be used for deriving a meaningful inference or result.

5.7.3 VANET Simulation

There are two kinds of simulation available in market. First is the time-dependent simulation and second is the time-independent simulation. The time-dependent simulation uses simulation clock and sets to some defined time and then keeps track of time and stops when simulation timer reaches the given threshold. Time-dependent simulation is subdivided into two parts: time-driven simulation and event-driven simulation.

- **Time-driven simulation:** In time-driven simulation, there is a fixed time interval as time threshold. Here, simulation keeps executing till simulation clock time reaches the given time threshold. In this simulation, events are executed at a predefined time interval during simulator life time.

5.7.3.1 Event-Driven Simulation

In event-driven simulator, a sequence of events occur at the simulator. There is no fixed time to trigger an event. Sequence of event is important. The simulation moves from one event to another event until simulation terminates. Time-driven simulator follows a chronological order, whereas in event-driven simulation, every new event is scheduled into the event list, which must be tagged with a time stamp equal to or greater than that of the current event. No outdated events can be scheduled. Second, event with the smallest time stamp in the event list is selected for execution. It will never jump over chronologically ordered events or jump back to the past event.

5.7.4 VANET-SIM

It is a java-based simulator developed for vehicular network simulation. VANET simulator is an easy way to simulate different scenarios in VANET with different parameters. Important features of VANET-SIM (Vsim) are listed as follows:

- **Security:** It strongly supports different concept in security. It provides an easy way to test different security concept in the vehicular network using VANET Simulator.
- **Platform independence:** As simulator is developed in JAVA 6 and JAVA is a platform independent, VANET Simulator is also platform independent and supports different system.
- **Extensibility:** Source code is written in JAVA. Therefore, different packages and classes can be easily extended to impart our own algorithm and functionality.
- **Realistic maps:** VANET Simulator provides an easy interface to import maps from the OpenStreetMap project. Real road maps can be easily uploaded in the simulator. It makes available to upload the existing map or user can create their own map as per requirements and upload.
- **Extensive scenario and map editor:** VANET Simulator provides a powerful editor facility to create new map or to edit the existing maps. User can upload different scenarios of traffic situation on already-uploaded map. Simulator also supports creation and configuration of scenarios and simulation runs.

- **Visualization:** VANET Simulator provides usable, easy graphical user interface. It gives different controlling tabs like add or delete vehicle, speed control, zoom-in and zoom-out tabs etc. A command line interface for high-performance simulation is available as well.
- **Microsimulation:** Simulator has a facility to edit each and every instance of object/entities. Considering an example of vehicle, the user can set individual vehicle attributes. The vehicle has its own unique ID, speed, range, and direction. Like a vehicle object, user can set attribute values of every object from VANET Simulator.
- **Integration of privacy-enhancing technologies**
  To do the empiric analysis of different traffic situations in vehicular ad hoc network, four techniques are implemented: mix zones, promix zones, silent periods, and slow.

5.7.5 Installation and Start

Installation steps for VANET Simulator (Vsim):

1. Download the Quick start pack of Vsim.
2. (http://svs.informatik.uni-hamburg.de/vanet/).
3. Extract the zip file, and click "VanetSimStarter.jar" to start the GUI-mode.
4. For simulations with a large amount of vehicles, the simulator should be started with the java ram option.
5. java-Xmx2048m-jar VanetSimStarter.jar. For quick simulations, the simulator can also be started in console-mode java-Xmx6144m-jar VanetSimStarter.jar map_file.xml scenario_file.xml 1000000 using the parameters: map, scenario, and simulation time.
6. You can test the simulator by opening a map file (e.g., Berlin_noTS.xml in the Quickstart-Pack) and a scenario file (e.g., Berlin_noTS_5000vehicles_withMix-Zones.xml in the Quickstart-Pack) and clicking the start button (see "The simulation tab" section for further information about starting your first simulation)
   - **The simulation tab:** Map with different tab on simulator is explained. Each tab on simulator is shown by numbers from 1 to 7. Use and meaning of tabs are explained in sequence of 1–7 (Figure 5.1).

1. **Map**: Uploaded map in current scenario of simulator.
2. Open map button to open a VANET Simulator map (transformed from an open street map in the edit mode).
3. Open Scenario button to open a scenario file which contains information about vehicles, mix zones, RSUs...
4. These arrow buttons are used to navigate your map, left, right, up or down.
5. These buttons are used to start, pause simulations, or jump to a specific time.
6. These checkboxes are used to view further information of vehicle like vehicle IDs, mix zones, and Wi-Fi radius.
7. This tab gives in detail information about map and vehicles in text box.

- **The edit tab** (Figure 5.2):
  1. User can create new maps by clicking on this button
  2. User can use this button to create a new scenario
  3. To save a map
  4. To save a scenario
  5. Import an open street map (OpenStreetMap-Project) and transform it into a VANET Simulator map
  6. This button opens the vehicle-type dialog. Vehicle types are used to create different types of vehicles very fast.
  7. This dropdown menu includes all important tools to create maps and scenarios. Create vehicles, RSUs, mix zones, silent-periods or change scenario settings like logging, communication timings, or create and change maps.

- **The report tab** (Figure 5.3):
  1. A summary of the running simulation like created messages, vehicle amount...
  2. Monitor beacons in a specific area.
  3. These buttons include different attacks on privacy concepts.

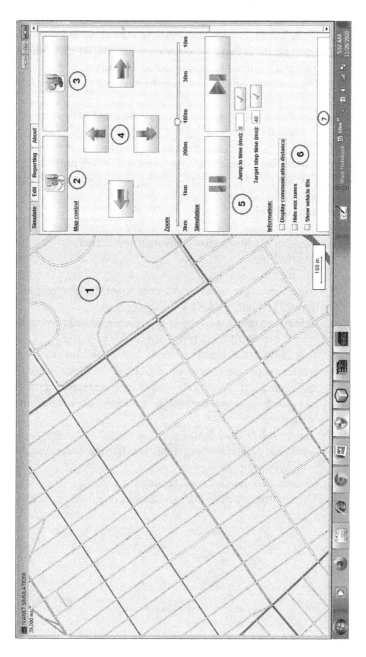

FIGURE 5.1 Map with simulation tab.

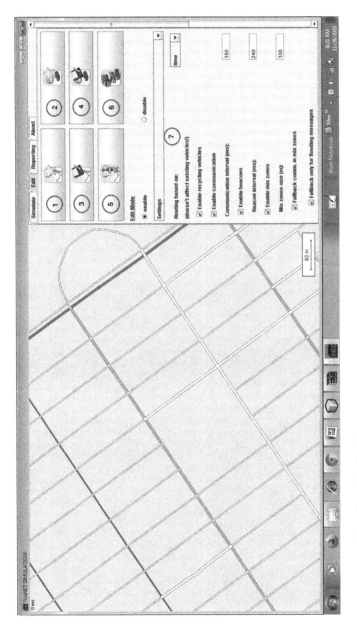

FIGURE 5.2 Map with edit tab in simulator.

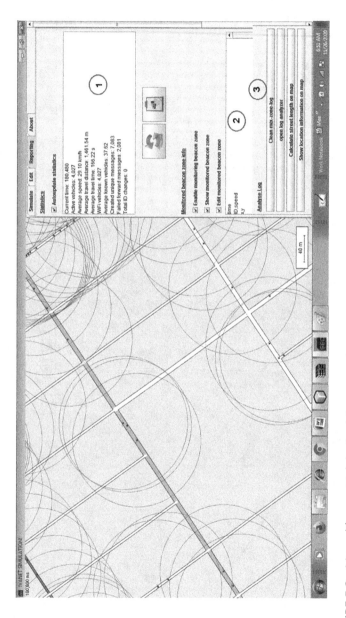

FIGURE 5.3 Map with report tab in simulator.

REFERENCES

1. T. Ishiyama, "Introduction to JARI", In *1st Asia Automobile Institute Summit*, Japan, Tokyo, 2012.
2. M. S. Akbar and C. M. A. Rashe, "VANETs Architectures and Protocol Stacks: A Survey", In *Proceedings of the Third International Conference on Communication Technologies for Vehicles*, 1970.
3. D. Manoj and B. G. B. Narendra, "Traffic congestion detection by using VANETs to improve intelligent transportation system (ITS)," *International Journal of Networks and Communications*, vol. 5, no. 4, pp. 74–82, 2015.
4. P. S. Ghode and R. Pochhi, "Vanet based intelligent road traffic monitoring and management system," *International Journal of Research in Advent Technology*, vol. 4, 2015.
5. J. Bhatia, R. Davea, H. Bhayani, S. Tanwar, and A. Nayyar, "SDN-based real-time urban traffic analysis in VANETs environment", Elsevier B.V., pp. 162–175, 1 2020.
6. S. A. Ben Mussa, M. Manaf, K. Z. Ghafoor, and Z. Doukha, "Simulation tools for vehicular ad hoc networks: A comparison study and future perspectives", In *2015 International Conference on Wireless Networks and Mobile Communications (WINCOM)*, Marrakech, pp. 1–8, 2015. doi:10.1109/WINCOM.2015.7381319.
7. S. Najafzadeh and N. B. Ithnin, "Broadcasting in connected and fragmented vehicular ad hoc networks", *International Journal of Vehicular Technology*, vol. 2014, pp. 1–15, 2014. Article ID 969076.

Conclusions

6

6.1 VEHICULAR AD HOC NETWORK

Road transportation is the heart of economic development of a country. Management of traffic services and their effective utilization have a direct impact on successful development of business and other domains in countries [1]. Providing vehicles with communication facility gives ample benefit to overcome many issues on road transportation. It can be used to priorly inform drivers about road conditions, traffic jams, accidents happened, weather conditions, front and side distances of other vehicles, sudden break applied by the preceding vehicle, or sudden obstacles in the path. All this safety information is used for analysis and further to react as per the result of analysis. Along with safety and security of drivers, the network facilitates information like map of a city, important locations in the city, paths from the source to the destination, and multimedia data like entertainment movie [2].

VANET (vehicular ad hoc network) research is at the peak; it has opened various options to the road traffic management and services on road. Developed countries are quite ahead in researching and implementing vehicular network and services. In developing countries like India, this network can be useful to tackle traffic management issues and toll plaza traffic jams by providing an easy way to identify vehicles, deduct tolls, and reduce road accidents.

This book provides a journey of VANET development. To establish VANET network, we should be aware with its basic components, communication medium for network, and different protocols used for communication. The first two chapters provides an introductory part of VANET, what is meant by ad hoc network, and discusses about different types of ad hoc networks, comparison of VANET with other ad hoc networks, scenario in VANET, components in VANET, and characteristics of VANET. These chapters also cover different communication methods and protocols used for communication in VANET.

Message forwarding is an important task for the network that exists. In the vehicular network, messages play important roles compared to any other network as they deal with runtime behaviors on road. As we have seen, there are different types of messages in VANET; it is a challenging task to decide importance of message and to assign priority to it for transmitting messages at the individual node [2]. Chapter 3 gives a relevance-based message forwarding scheme where messages are categorized as per importance. Messages are assigned with priority, and they are transmitted based on message's trust value and relevance value [1].

VANET is the most volatile and open network; there is no any control on the movement of nodes in the network. A new node can easily enter into the network, which may raise a security issue. Due to this feature, VANET is prone to many challenges like volatility, critical time latency of messages delivery, high mobility of nodes, VANET security, efficient message forwarding, and mitigation techniques to address VANET security [3–5]. These challenges are discussed in Chapter 4.

6.2 VANET AND INTELLIGENT TRANSPORTATION SYSTEM

Human beings are intelligent animals due to their special abilities. We can think, and we can take decisions; we can compare things, and we can easily learn new things. Intelligent systems are developed by imparting the same intelligence. Any decision system is based on data acquired from the environment and its analyses according to some previous experiences or rule theory. VANET uses the same principle; different environmental sensors and devices are deployed on the vehicle, which collect different parameter at runtime, process it, and give decisions to the control unit. Decisions can be disseminated for control action in vehicle itself or for other vehicles alert [2]. Processing data effectively is another domain of research, which is not widely considered in this book.

Vehicular network provides an intelligent transportation system. As we discussed, different messages and their importance are given in Section 3.2. These messages are generated based on the data collected and the analysis made by on-board units (OBUs). Intelligent transportation system mainly considers the following services that are discussed in Chapter 5. It provides road safety, traffic management, user-oriented services, and convenience services [6].

Intelligent transportation system will result in an effective traffic management with less human resources. It will avoid unnecessary traffic jams. It will prevent accidents due to different traffic scenarios and environmental parameters. It can be helpful for smart toll collection and faulty vehicle detections. Currently, we do not have actual data from the real-time scenario on road, which can give a conclusion about how much time and money can be saved by deploying VANET. It needs a full-fledge deployment of VANET and daily measurement of performance.

6.3 FUTURE OF VANET

VANET is developed under an ad hoc network with distinct features. Most of the research is tested and implemented on various available simulators. Some of the developed countries are implementing test bed and deploying VANET infrastructure. In future, VANET has a wide scope in services on road and acts as a road assistant for user to recommend different services, and to provide navigation, emergency messages, etc.

6.3.1 Developed Countries

VANET is partially deployed in developed countries with limited services. They establish basic infrastructure while road construction. Road side units are part of road infrastructure. Vehicles are equipped with OBUs. Trusted authority is responsible for monitoring, registration, and other admin activities. Developed countries are researching on the enhancement of communication, security, and speeding message forwarding in the vehicular network. They are trying to develop services, which can be possible with the help of VANET. Research organizations from developed countries, like CARLINK Consortium, implemented a platform. Under this platform, cars are made available with updates regarding weather conditions, urban traffic management, and different information of city. WiSafeCar comes up with a project in VANET. The overall aim of this project is to provide reliable traffic services to vehicles. It mainly focuses on traffic safety alert messages like accidents that have happened, traffic jams, and other data services to vehicles. SAFESPOT project on autonomous vehicle-based safety systems is limited by the field of view of their sensors. Cooperative systems using communication between vehicles and infrastructure can considerably enhance this field of view, thus leading to a breakthrough for road safety.

6.3.2 Developing Countries

Research is carried out using a simulator that needs to prove on test bed with actual environment. As discussed in this book, developing countries are using VANET network to improve traffic management system, reduce accident, avoid traffic jam situation, and provide other services. To establish a vehicular network is the first challenge in these countries. Cost of deployment, selecting frequency spectrum, and deciding and developing protocols for VANET working are also prior goals in these countries. The existing research work, which has been already proven with simulators and small test bed, needs to be implemented in a real-world road scenario, which is also the future scope in VANET.

REFERENCES

1. S. P. Godse, P. N. Mahalle, et al., "Rising issues in VANET communication and security: A state of art survey", *International Journal of Advanced Computer Science and Applications*, vol. 8, no. 9, pp. 245–252, 2017.
2. S. P. Godse, P. N. Mahalle, et al., "Priority-based message-forwarding scheme in VANET with intelligent navigation", *Applied Machine Learning for Smart Data Analysis* (Eds., N. Dey, P. N. Mahalle, M. S. Pathan, S. Wagh), pp. 169–182. CRC Press, Boca Raton, FL, March 2019.
3. S. P. Godse, P. N. Mahalle, "A computational analysis of ECC based novel authentication scheme in VANET", *International Journal of Electrical and Computer Engineering (IJECE)*, vol. 8, no. 6, pp. 5268–5277, December 2018.
4. S. Goudarzi and A. H. Abdullah, "A systematic review of security in vehicular ad hoc network", *In the 2nd Symposium on Wireless Sensors and Cellular Networks (WSCN'13)*, 2013.
5. S. P. Godse and P. N. Mahalle, "Intelligent authentication and message forwarding in VANET". *International Journal of Smart Vehicles and Smart Transportation (IJSVST)*, vol. 3, no. 1, pp. 1–20, 2020. doi:10.4018/IJSVST.2020010101.
6. M. E. Zorkany and A. Yasser, "Vehicle to vehicle "V2V" communication: Scope, importance, challenges, research directions and future", *The Open Transportation Journal*, vol. 14, no. 2, pp. 86–98, 2020.

Index

Printed in the United States
by Baker & Taylor Publisher Services